TO THE RIVER KWAI

THE DEATH RAILWAY

415 km long

688 bridges (of which 8 'permanent' steel w/concrete piers)

Built July 1942 to October 1943 by:
P.O.W.s 61,106
Asiatic coolies 182,948

Estimated deaths 150,000

0   20   40   60   80   100 km

THAILAND (SIAM)

Gulf of Siam

TO THE RIVER KWAI

TWO JOURNEYS – 1943, 1979

JOHN STEWART

BLOOMSBURY

First published in 1988
Copyright © 1988 by Spark SA
Reprinted December 1988

Bloomsbury Publishing Ltd, 2 Soho Square,
London W1V 5DE

British Library Cataloguing in Publication Data

Stewart, John
To the River Kwai: two journeys, 1943,
1979
1. Burma. Kwai River region. Description
& travel. Biographies
I. Title
915.91′045

ISBN 0-7475-0297-8

Typeset by Columns of Reading
Printed in Great Britain by
Butler & Tanner Ltd, Frome and London

TO THOSE WHO DIDN'T MAKE IT
OUT OF SONKURAI AND TAMBAYA

John Stewart was born in England in 1919, educated in France, and worked briefly on the London Stock Exchange before going off for a six-year stint in the British Army. Speaking perfect French and some Arabic, he was sent to Singapore four weeks before surrender. As a P.O.W. he learned Japanese, and worked as interpreter on the River Kwai.

The war over, Stewart took up photography in New York. Success came quickly with publication in fashion magazines and with important advertising commissions. But in the Sixties he moved back to Europe – to France and Switzerland.

In spite of his disastrous first encounter with Asia, the pull is "East of Suez": in 1958 Stewart was technical adviser to David Lean in Sri Lanka where the celebrated *Bridge on the River Kwai* was shot; in '79 he was the first ex-P.O.W. to make his way back to the upper reaches of the Kwai; the year '81 was spent photographing and trekking in Ladakh; he has published a book about an elephant school in Thailand; and more recently he visited remote (and forbidden) Amdo in north-east Tibet.

Stewart now devotes much of his time to producing black-and-white photographic still-lifes which have been exhibited in over fifty museum and gallery one-man shows.

CONTENTS

FOREWORD

Not a day has gone by that, triggered by a relevance, sometimes pertinent, often irrational, I haven't thought of the river and the camps around the Three Pagodas. These thoughts are not, you understand, in the nature of reflections, lessons to be drawn from the past, or meditations concerning the nature of man. They are ephemeral views, side glimpses and disembodied images, as distant and yet as tenacious as would be, if we could imagine it, memories of a past incarnation.

This book might, for all I know, be an attempt to put order over these random and persistent reminiscences. Its aim is certainly not to exorcise the past, for that particular past has been of enormous value.

What has made this memoir possible forty-five years after the event are the notes that I kept from April to December 1943, the nine months I spent on the Siam-Burma Railway. It's the only time of my captivity that I did so, and I don't know what prompted the decision. I remember, however, how difficult it was to find scraps of paper and to keep them dry during the monsoon. As soon as we returned to Singapore, I typed these notes on the back of Japanese roll-call forms, and destroyed the originals.

The typewritten pages are still here by my side, increasingly brittle and yellow; alongside a chess set made of teakwood with pieces whittled out of bamboo; my army knife; a Japanese "course in the spoken language" (approved by the Military Propaganda Dept., Kuala Lumpur) with sentences such as "This ship cannot be sunk by torpedoes" and "Please do not put oil in my hair"; and my Soldier's Service and Pay Book in the name of Lance Corporal John Stewart Ullmann, for such is the lowly rank (except for a temporary plateau as Acting Sergeant) that I managed to achieve after being in His Majesty's service from June 1939 to November 1945.

As a professional photographer – my life's work – I used my middle name to sign my pictures and my books. This is why the author of this memoir is John Stewart, although the author of the diary was only known at the time as John Ullmann.

The names of our camps underwent wonderful transformations, from their Thai version to the Japanese and English transliterations. For the sake of consistency I have used the research of Captain C.E. Escritt, who has compiled the most authoritative historical study of the railway. Philip Reed at the Imperial War Museum was a great help with research. Thanks (and admiration) go to my agent, Dasha Shenkman, who agreed to handle, at this enormous remove of almost a half century, yet another manuscript of the Second World War.

J.S., 1988

TO THE RIVER KWAI

PROLOGUE

(1979)

Volutes of grey mist seep from the Chao Phraya's tepid waters into the halls of Noi Station. As the first rays of the sun slip through the roof girders, the mist turns salmon pink. In Bangkok this is the best moment of the day – calm, cool and voluptuous.

The station is silent. It's six in the morning, the trains are immobile. No clang of bumping and coupling; no brakes squealing and engines whistling. The only insistent sound comes from the passengers' rubber flip-flops as they smack the concrete. I'm reminded of pigeons' wings clacking under the great glass canopies of European railway terminals, of other journeys and of other dawns.

The passengers are mostly country folk. Their empty baskets, tied to long bamboo poles, are lined up along the platforms: the ducks and the fishes, the papayas and the brinjals have been sold in the city markets, and it's time to return to the attap-roofed houses along the paddy fields. Squatting on their heels, the peasants wait for the carriage doors to be unbolted.

Sitting on a wooden bench, I too wait for a train.

So far I haven't been tempted to extract from the canvas bag at my feet yesterday's *Bangkok Times* or the paperback bought a few days ago in Tokyo. Ineluctable hours spent in the bus, rail and air terminals of Asia have long ago taught me that the most effective solace against boredom is the observation of *Homo Asiaticus* in his many variants.

A flock of raven-black Karens is hulking down around the ticket-booth. They're the best mahouts in Thailand, these Karens: no one understands elephants the way they do. I got to know them

1

a year ago, when I was photographing them working with their great beasts in the teak forests along the Laos border.

Hill-tribes belong in the hills or inside the pages of the *National Geographic*. Here the blue tracery of tattoos over their faces, chests and limbs looks incongruous. Men and women pull at long-stemmed pipes. The children, stunned by the smoke of the black cheroots they're given as pacifiers, huddle together against the cold.

In the half light a splotch of Buddhist orange suddenly appears and hovers above them like a low cloud. The Karens shuffle sideways on their heels to let a monk go through. Frustrated in his attempt to buy a ticket (the booth is not yet opened for business), he turns around and walks away. His fleshy face is almost masked by oversize, aviator-style sunglasses. A small boy, also dressed in sacerdotal orange, follows on his heels. With his left hand the boy drags a heavy bundle, while the right is furiously engaged in nose-picking.

Together they stop and contemplate a poster. In a curious photomontage, a bridge has been grafted on to a pagoda. The poster is promoting a cheap, one-day excursion ticket to the *Chedi* at Nakhon Pathom, the tallest stupa in the country, with a trip to the River Kwai. *See The Death Railway – Visit the Cemeteries*, reads the copy in both Thai and English.

The monk and the boy sit on a bench close to mine. A man I take to be a beggar approaches them. Eyes lowered, he holds out his hands in the supplicant's gesture, then drops to the ground and prostrates himself until his head touches the monk's right shoe. But he's not a beggar, for from his thin cotton jacket he extracts two plastic bags containing beans in a saffron sauce. He offers them, eyes down and arms extended. The boy takes them. A short nod of the monk's shaven head at the same time thanks and dismisses the donor.

An official in the uniform of the Thai State Railways comes towards me. He is quite young. He bows and smiles. Could we speak together, he wants to know: he wishes to practise his English. His khaki drill tropicals have been ironed with such precision, creased into so many knife-edges, that he looks like a Cubist painting. Even the colour, raw sienna, is right.

"Where you from?" he asks.

"From England."

"Where you going?"

"To Kanchanaburi, and then on to Nam Tok," I answer.

"Ah, Nam Tok. Very interesting journey. And you know, the train is very slow but very safe. *Mai pen rai.*"

The national mantra literally translated means, It doesn't matter. You hear it incessantly, and it should indicate extreme caution, for what has been dismissed as being of no importance will be certain, on the contrary, to matter a great deal. In this instance what is really being said is, Do not worry. What the young man can't know is that I'm the possessor of arcane knowledge and I don't have to be reassured: there is indeed nothing to fear, nothing to worry about. Lightning never strikes the same tree twice, or an artillery shell the same hole. Here, in this country, on this stretch of railway, so much once happened to me that according to that law of no double-strike, by dint of an identical necessity, the future, I am certain, holds no further catastrophe.

I can't resist an effect, and I throw away my lines. "Yes, I know. I've worked on that railway."

"Ah, then, you are a railway engineer?"

"No," I answer, "it was during the war – the Second World War. I was a prisoner then."

My companion is silent. Diffidently, like a hesitant lover, he lets the tip of his index finger stroke the back of my hand. He looks into my face: Westerners can become angry when you touch them without permission. Then, tenderly, he enfolds my hand in both his, and he says, "I congratulate you. You are still alive."

So started my second journey up the River Kwai.

I

GETTING THERE

ONE

The concatenation of events that brought me back in 1979 to Thailand and the River Kwai could be traced back to a point whose initial coordinates would read: "Time: November 1938. Place: the London Stock Exchange." The line is of unusual length, the consequence of my inveterate love of travel.

If I now offer to produce an autobiographical fragment, if I propose to exhibit a shard of my life labelled "Kwai, 1943", it's also necessary, I imagine, to offer some information concerning provenance.

Let it be briefly said, then, that I was born into a vast clan that found its ethos in the combined rigours of Victorian puritanism and a Judaic sense of dedication. For puritanism, read stoic avoidance of all emotion; and for dedication, substitute duty. The result was, in its lesser aspects, stifling. In its worst it produced sadistic tendencies, such as a propensity for practical jokes that could inflict considerable mental suffering. If I managed to escape suffocation I owe it mostly to the accident of having been brought up in France.

My grandfather on my mother's side was David Gestetner, the inventor of the duplicating machine and the founder of the company that was started over a century ago in the City of London. He was stern and didactic. In the course of a walk in a London park, I remember him picking up a bird feather, and explaining, with a lucidity that must have left a mark on a very small boy's mind, why a tube was stronger than a solid rod. I can also conjure up his impassive face as he listened on the wireless, as it was then called, to one of Hitler's speeches. This must have been in the early thirties. I asked him the meaning of these German words spewed out by the raucous, passionate voice. "War, inevitably," he answered, without comment, and without a trace of emotion on his features.

He had emigrated to England from Hungary. (Via Chicago, where the only work he was given by the Hungarian Aid Society was selling Japanese paper kites. There was no future in America, was his conclusion.) He married Sophie Lazarus, who came from an old Anglo-Jewish family. She was even more stern than her husband, and her influence is still felt nightly when I take my shoes off. I was sleeping in my grandparents' house (at the probable age of five or six) when she woke me up, ordered me out of bed and instructed me to align my shoes in the approved fashion; I had deposited them outside my room to be polished, but in such a way that the toes pointed outwards – in other words, the right shoe was on the left side, and the left on the right.

My grandfather, among his other qualities, must have possessed a singular intuition. His son-in-law, my father, who was the head of Gestetner in France, once remarked to him that naturally one day I would take over from him the management of the French business. "That won't be," said my grandfather, "John will never work for the firm. He is the artist among us." I was then four years old.

The oracle was, of course, disregarded. My father, in any case, was used to having his way. If he was able to exercise considerable charm over his friends, towards members of his family his attitude was nothing less than tyrannical. He identified himself with the Jehovah of the Old Testament who simultaneously holds out tremendous rewards and hideous punishments depending on whether the Children of Israel bide his words or negate his will. The Orthodox ritual of Judaism always ruled my father's household. From a very early age on, I considered it to be an incomprehensible tribal charade. It repelled me.

One of the very few times that I was moved by my father was when he admitted that he had never had any intimation of a godhead; or heard an echo which might have come from beyond the horizon of *l'homme moyen sensuel*. "Unlike you," he said, "art doesn't speak to me. And if I didn't go through the ritual you hate so much, I would be nothing but a crass human being." So the incomprehensible charade was not even Pascal's famous bet – there is no proof of the existence of God, but if He does exist then a lifetime of devotional acts would not have been in vain.

What my father was doing was utterly gratuitous, a challenge to common sense. More: a challenge to the principle of causality – a proof no less that all our acts need not be for the sake of a return or a reward.

So convinced were my parents that I would become precisely what my grandfather said I would not, that instead of being sent back to England for my schooling, I went to a private elementary school in Paris, the Cour Lacascade, and then on to the Lycée Janson in the XVIth Arrondissement where we lived.

Janson de Sailly (site of the first potato field in France under Louis XV) was a notoriously bad school, snobbish and very right-wing. The threat of Fascism and of Nazi Germany was eclipsed by the horror of the Soviet Union and the terror of Communism in Europe. Every student was urged to join a political group. As a British subject, I could not expect full rank, but I was granted membership, *à titre étranger,* in Colonel de la Roque's Croix-de-Feu. Somewhat to the left of the lunatic Right – it never collaborated with the Germans during the Occupation – the Colonel's organisation was not anti-semitic.

Weekends were action time. Dressed in riding clothes (regardless of whether I was riding or not), I swaggered down the Avenue du Bois, now Avenue Foch. The Croix-de-Feu badge was inserted back-to-front in the lapel of my hacking jacket. Whenever I met a rival right-winger, such as a Camelot du Roi, a follower of the royalist party, I flipped the lapel of my jacket, thus exposing my badge and revealing my true political affiliations. My would-be adversary then flashed his fleur-de-lys badge, and we would tribalistically snarl at each other.

These minutiae of my adolescence would not be worth recollecting if it were not for the fact that they reveal a lack of shape, an absence of passion and an aimlessness that I now find truly incomprehensible. I was certainly not part of the *jeunesse dorée*, of the "happy few" in their English version. Unlike my schoolfellow Murat, there was no Rolls-Royce to collect me from Janson at four p.m. to drive me to the golf course at St Cloud. I rode home on my bike. Whatever might have been the material privileges of my existence, the family's puritanical ethos discouraged frivolity. Yet my father was fastidious to a point. His cars in the twenties had to have genuine cane-weave on the doors. By his bedside stood a

Baccarat glass of such fragility that no maid could be entrusted to wash it; the task fell to my mother. No handkerchief had ever been made with a hand-rolled hem thin enough to please him. Occasionally we heard echoes of the tongue-lashings his tailor or his barber had to endure.

My mother, on the other hand, seemed possessed of a social conscience. She recalled the pain, when she was a small girl, of seeing the female domestics in her parents' house hauling buckets of hot water to the top floors, and she thought the trade unions were "a good thing". In Paris, she had washbasins with hot and cold running water installed in the squalid rooms the servants occupied under the roof, thus making enemies among her friends who feared that "the rot would spread".

Her frivolous side was expressed through gambling. She adored casinos. Probably she needed excitement. There's certainly no other explanation for her behaviour on the night of February 6, 1934, when the Right went on the rampage in Paris, attempting to overthrow the government and destroy parliamentary democracy. Mobs were milling around the Place de la Concorde, and the black-uniformed Gardes Mobiles were out in full battle gear. The revolutionary virus, endemic in France, was causing a high fever to run in the body politic. My father was away on a business trip, so my mother and I, after listening to the radio, went to see the show.

The roars of the crowd sounded like the surging of the tide. Rifle fire broke out, sharp and staccato, from the direction of the Chambre des Députés. Roars became shouts. A tidal wave of bodies flowed away from the shooting. Holding hands, we too ran off towards the Champs Elysées, to the the shelter of the chestnut trees in front of the American Embassy.

It must have been the same genes which, when I was living the life of a lotus-eater in Gstaad, caused me to leave family and chalet, to get into my car and drive to Paris in order to be part of *les Evènements* of May 1968 – the French students' uprising. My poor wife's incomprehension in the face of such irresponsibility must have been as great as my father's anger when he learned how his wife and son had spent that night.

After passing my *baccalauréat*, the crowning exam of French secondary education, the time came to leave home for good. It was the tail-end of a summer spent in the Normandy country house my parents rented every year. My mother looked serious. "John," she said, "I don't think you have been terribly well prepared to face life on your own. We have one more day ahead of us. Tomorrow morning you will be taught to iron a pair of trousers; and in the afternoon cook will show you how to make a decent omelette."

Thus equipped, I went to Manchester to take up the life of a navvy. This came about because I didn't think I was in the least suited to university studies, and it was decided on my behalf, as I was rudderless, that I should go into the oil business.

This *ad hoc* decision was further motivated by, firstly, my refusal to have anything to do with Gestetner and its ideals of "salesmanship" elevated to one of the highest virtues known to man; and, secondly, by a most unlikely commercial transaction in which one of my uncles happened to be involved financially. During the last months of the year 1937, Hitler's ravings (his "last demand") thundered over the European continent. The countries likely to be involved in the forthcoming conflict were accelerating their preparedness. England, among its other needs, was deficient in specialised lubricating oils. Germany had both the know-how and the machinery to produce them. German Jews had the money. A three-way arrangement was struck, whereby the plant would be funded, probably at a huge premium, by German Jews who would be repaid in Sterling if they had managed to emigrate to Britain. German industry would build, ship and instal the complete refinery in Manchester; and finally, British tanks and aircraft would be adequately lubricated for the impending contest.

By the time I got to the Manchester Oil Refinery, the foundation work had been started. A team of German technicians under the command of a slim, ultra-blonde, hard-faced young female engineer, had arrived with part of the plant. The boss-woman was always dressed in black and wore hunting boots. Over her left nipple (hard and light pink, I was sure) she had alluringly pinned a discreet swastika. All she needed to complete the outfit was a bullwhip. I found her desperately attractive but she was unapproachable. I had no option but to unload my excess libido on her exact opposite, a smooth and fleshy Lancashire girl with no style at all, but with big, solid breasts, a broad bum and an equally broad Mancunian accent. She was really a poor substitute for the sexual attraction known as *le goût de l'étranger*. Her successor was an American woman, much older than I was, whom I called Chouchoute because she came from Chatanooga, Tennessee, home of the choo-choo. But I couldn't help being mentally unfaithful to these girls: the Nazi boss-woman was irreplaceable.

The only contribution I could make to the refinery under construction in the industrial area along the Manchester Ship Canal known as Trafford Park, a true example of the "dark, satanic mills", was physical strength. I was apprenticed to a squad of seven men: two welders – one electric, one acetylene – two fitters and three navvies. The work was hard, digging ditches in the muddy soil, laying pipes and connecting them with heavy flanges. Very soon I was told that I was not an apprentice any more but a fully fledged navvy. My connection with management was of course known, but no one ever referred to it, addressed me in a heavy ironic manner, or tried to unload on me his hate of the capitalist owners. Perhaps the class struggle was dormant in Lancashire. I attribute the fact that I was left in peace mainly to having faced successfully the tea test. Five or six times daily, the squad stopped work, filled their billy-cans with water and scraped into them the treacly contents of a newspaper screw. These screws contained a rich mixture of black tea leaves, sugar and sweet condensed milk. They were prepared daily by the men's wives, along with "chip butties", greasy cold french fries sandwiched between two slabs of bread. The acetylene welder brought the billy-cans to a boil until the mix, which always included fragments of the *Daily Mirror* was hot enough to scald. I yet have to decide whether that tea ordeal was better or worse than two others I had to face in the course of my life: one was British Army hospital tea so thick you could stand a spoon in it; and the other Tibetan buttered tea (the butter always slightly rancid), salty and lukewarm, where the *Daily Mirror* fragments are often replaced by a shiny black yak hair.

I didn't last long in Manchester. Hedonism got the better of me. Industry having failed, it was thought that merchant-banking in the City of London would be more congenial. Once again, the bank was found that would take me on. My future employers, however, wanted me to have a grounding in the practices of the Stock Exchange. I was therefore farmed out to friendly stockbrokers.

Before being admitted to the *sanctum sanctorum*, the floor of the "House", as the Stock Exchange in Throgmorton Street was known, I had to appear before an admission panel composed of large and sombre men seated around a horseshoe table. Overly varnished portraits of what I took to be Founding Fathers of the House hung behind them on the wood-panelled walls. I was made to stand in the U of the horseshoe, and answer questions quite unrelated to the career I proposed to enter. What school did I go to? What games did I play? Did I shoot? Did I ride to hounds? I was asked to leave the room while Mr Stokes, my future employer, stayed behind. When, a few minutes later, I faced the panel once again, the chairman sternly said, "Don't make a fool of yourself." This meant that I was accepted, and that I should make quite sure not to be caught with my hand in the till.

Over a glass of champagne in one of the many underground bars around Throgmorton Street, Mr Stokes explained the rules. I was always to wear a stiff collar. A fresh carnation in the lapel of my coat was, at my age, more suitable than a rose; anyway, if you wore a rose, then it had better be from your own garden. And under no circumstances was I ever to sit down in the House: the few seats were reserved for the very old members who used the Stock Exchange as a place to get away from their wives. I felt very far away from my mates toiling along the Manchester Ship Canal.

Although I could now enter the precincts of the House, I belonged to the lowest caste entitled to that privilege. I was known as a Blue Button, and such was the badge I wore next to my carnation renewed every morning at a City florist on my way to the House. But the very first step in my new life was to make the rounds of the porters who stood at the various street entrances of the Stock Exchange so that they could have a good look at me. These porters, known as "waiters" because stock trading started in coffee houses, were recruited for their phenomenal memory for faces. Whenever the call "Stranger in the House!" went up (this happened generally once a year, and all trading stopped), it meant that a waiter had failed in his calling.

A Blue Button was not allowed to trade, neither on his own behalf or on his employers'. All he could do was ask questions. He was bullied, mocked, ordered about, and if he idly stood around reading a newspaper, someone was sure to creep up with a lighted match and set it ablaze. In brief, the future member of the London Stock Exchange found himself back to his first years in a typical English public school, treated like a new boy. I didn't mind it in the least: I could not be said to be leading a stressful life. Work didn't start before ten, and by three thirty I was on my way home to a tiny studio in Highgate Village. There, in a futuristic block of flats, I could swim, play squash or tennis until the time came to cross the street to a pub where it was said that Dick Whittington (and cat) heard the Bow Bells calling him back to London.

No sooner had I joined the House than I found myself in uniform. An old friend of my family was the Honorary Colonel of an officer-producing unit of the Territorial Army, which was solely composed of volunteers. Roughly a third of the three hundred men of 332 Company, Royal Engineers, came from the Stock Exchange; another third from the Inns of Court; the remainder were minor peers and baronets, racing men and business punters. The Hon. Colonel said I was to join 332 Company, and so I did. I was given a number, 2088658, and a First World War uniform with lots of brass buttons. I learned to polish them without dribbling Brasso on the khaki tunic, to blanco webbing, to roll puttees, and I got myself a dog bone in order to obtain a high shine on my regulation boots.

We manned anti-aircraft searchlights. One night a week we left our Albany Street barracks and drove our equipment to nearby Regent's Park. R.A.F. Reserve pilots flew slow and antiquated Tiger Moth planes which we attempted to illuminate. The problem of finding an aircraft in the night sky was supposedly solved by means of a sound locator. This curious device, which looked like a Tinguely sculpture, consisted of two pairs of trumpets arranged in a cross. Each pair was connected to the ears of a sapper (as Royal Engineers privates are called). As this machine was invented before the advent of mesons, quarks, bits and bytes, the principle is easy to follow: the sapper responsible for finding the altitude of the plane tilted his two trumpets, which were arranged one on top of the other, until the sound of the aircraft appeared to locate itself precisely in the very top of his skull. He then directed the three men on the searchlight itself to tilt it up or down until it was parallel with the trumpets. The same principle applied to the man in charge of finding the longitudinal position of the aircraft.

The trouble was that by the time the sound was centred inside one's cranium the plane had travelled quite a distance and the searchlight illuminated nothing. The only certain hits were scored on the bushes of Regent's Park; it was fun to try and place the grunts and the orgasmic pantings in the middle of one's head.

In June 1939, 332 Company went to Suffolk for a month, on an exercise named "coverture". It was, in fact, a form of semimobilisation. What I retain from this idyllic period is the admirable training I received in holding down prodigious quantities of whisky and ale at a pub called the Barley Mow in Little Yeldham.

Three weeks after my return to the House from the Barley Mow, I saw the number 27 light up on a certain panel high up between two columns. This meant that I was wanted on the telephone. This time it wasn't my firm's correspondents in Brussels or Paris. It was a ridiculously theatrical voice that uttered just two words 'Camden Arms'. This was the password to report to barracks immediately. Many other young men had received the same call. All trading stopped. An old troll of a jobber in the Kaffir Market, the South African gold mines, with a face like an apple long forgotten in a drawer, patted me on the shoulder. "I saw them go before, my boy. And I can tell by the look in their eyes if they'll come back or not. You will."

I returned to my flat, put on my uniform and took a taxi to the barracks. Albany Street was lined with London Transport buses that were to take us to our "war sites". However the crush of Lagondas, Bentleys, Rolls-Royces and Alvises – to mention only the stars – belonging to the sappers was such that the buses were told to go away empty. I was driven in a grey Jaguar S.S. to the village of Finchingfield in Essex.

TWO

We were nine men on our "war-site" under the command of a lance corporal. The equipment consisted of a large Lister diesel-electric lorry which served to generate electricity as well as to transport the crew, the searchlight and the sound locator. At first we were under canvas, but by the end of the summer a couple of Quonset huts were built for us at the edge of a field belonging to Home Farm, a mile from the village green.

Finchingfield was a sleepy, postcard-pretty village of white cottages with exposed timbers and thatched roofs. Among the owners of the more elegant of these cottages where we went to have hot baths was John Gielgud. On one side of the green and its duck-pond stood a classical Georgian brick house, and on the opposite, the local pub. The Georgian house was the bilious vicar's rectory; and in the pub's saloonbar a pretty sixteen-year-old prostitute, Finchingfield Flossie, could often be found waiting for trade. Flossie never knew what to make of us: we treated her like a deb.

We lived well. Packages arrived regularly from Fortnum's and from Harrods. Twice-monthly, Freibourg & Treyer in the Haymarket would mail me a supply of Turkish and Virginia cigarettes. In and out of season, the boys from Home Farm snared or shot pheasants. Our First World War uniforms were replaced by the new battledress, and I had my tailor on Dover Street run one up out of West of England cloth. As "other-ranks", i.e. non-officers, we didn't dare wear ties, but figured silk scarves were a proper substitute. When on leave, we wore brown shoes rather than the hideous black boots with their toecaps which turned upwards. Sadly, we were so often stopped by the Military Police ("You're improperly dressed! You're on a charge!"), that we gave up our improved, bespoke uniforms, and wore civvies.

In the search for style in an Anglian ploughed field, the prize went to the detachment five miles from us. A chef and two waiters from the Berkeley Hotel in Mayfair, along with food, plates and silver were called in to "do" for Christmas. Wives and girlfriends came down as well.

The winter of '39 was bitterly cold, and sentry duty at night particularly unpleasant. My madeleine for that winter is the smell of the kerosene heater over which we tried to get some feeling back in our hands after sentry duty (two hours on, four hours off), when we stood, cold and forlorn, in the middle of a ploughed field with a Lee-Enfield rifle slung over the shoulder. Once a week we were allowed a twenty-four-hour leave, and as I owned a diminutive Morris car, a 1927 two-seater tourer that I'd bought for £5 from a man suddenly posted to France, I motored up to London regularly. War, so far wasn't a shattering experience. It was the time that the French called *la drôle de guerre*.

With the spring of 1940, the war brutally ceased to be *drôle*. The idyllic weather became the hideous *Hitlerwetter* as Panzer squadrons raced over the sun-baked earth of Northern Europe, and the sun-filled skies reverberated with the passage of Stuka dive-bombers, Heinkels and Dorniers.

Paris fell. German armour struck south. The French Army collapsed. All was lost. I sat on a hill, my face turned east towards France, the country where I had been brought up, where I felt home to be. Where I imagined my parents and my two sisters fleeing from the invader. (They made their way to Bordeaux, whence they embarked for Plymouth.)

With me was a friend whose ancestors had arrived in England with William of Normandy. In the East Coast village where they had been given land in the 11th century, his family was still referred to by the locals as "the foreigners." As if in a somnambulistic state, I heard my friend say, "It's all over. France is done for."

The hurt inexplicably gave way to a great calm. The terrible events that were taking place only a few miles away, and in which I was playing no part except in the imagination, began to recede. I became conscious only of the sun's warmth, of the smells of the earth, and of the lark's clicking high above the hill in the pale Anglian sky. It was the present that mattered and the awareness of one's life. I was to feel this more than once in the course of the war, but on that spring day of 1940 I didn't understand the value or the role of the experience.

During the Battle of Britain and the subsequent night bombings, grief over France was swept away. France was dead, but Britain was alive. *"Ah Dieu que la guerre est jolie!"* Apollinaire had said a quarter of a century before. I was experiencing on a collective scale what I was to discover later at the personal level – the heady and secret joy of knowing you're alive while your comrades have died. As if you had been chosen to embody the victory of light over darkness.

Night after night, fleets of Luftwaffe bombers flew over our site at 10,000 feet. Catching a plane in the searchlight beam was as simple as throwing a net over a sleepy trout in a sunny pool. On clear nights, as simple as watching the pinpoints of starlight as they were blotted out by the passage of a squadron, and directing the beam on to them.

Once we caught a Stuka dive-bomber. The pilot dropped his aircraft straight down the beam. The screaming-devices on the wings produced a noise so shattering that you thought your teeth were going to fall out. I was Number Two on the searchlight itself. I pulled the switch, killed the light and peed in my trousers. The Stuka tore out of its dive and released one bomb. It impacted thirty yards away, bounced and exploded, causing no damage. Like the characters of fiction who have been emptied of feeling after a terrible sorrow, I felt nothing except the wetness between my legs getting cold. All the fear had been taken out of me. It was the last time; after that I would never again be rattled by gunfire.

Invasion was imminent. The searchlight sites along the East and South Coasts were to serve as the pivotal strongpoints between which the infantry (mostly the remnants that had come out of Dunkirk) would manoeuvre after the German forces had landed. We received fifty sandbags to build a pillbox for our 1916 Lewis gun which generally jammed after the first twenty rounds; two extra rifles (Canadian, 1911); and a case of Molotov cocktails (in bottles of Bass Pale Ale) to hurl at the Panzers.

The Luftwaffe switched to night bombing. The London docks went up in flames, and fifty miles away, on our site, we read the newspaper by the light of the fires.

The first item we scanned when we opened *The Times* was the King's List of Commissions. Often this was the first intimation that from gunner (we had been switched from the Engineers to Artillery), someone among us had been instantly elevated to the rank of second lieutenant in some posh regiment. Our old 332 Company started disintegrating, so when the Hon. Colonel came to see me at Home Farm, I told him how much I too would like to leave the searchlights and get into some more exciting form of warfare. Back in London the Hon. Colonel had tea with my mother and confirmed that within two weeks my commission would come through. Unfortunately the night before my papers arrived at H.Q., I ploughed the Commanding Officer's car into a deep ditch. The C.O. cursed me from the back seat; it was his personal vehicle, not Army Issue. He refused to sign the papers, and even the King himself couldn't have done anything about it. I thought it wise to ask for a transfer and, I suspect not entirely by chance, I found myself in Carlisle as a searchlight instructor in a dismal training camp.

Once more, family connections came to my rescue. While on leave in Sussex in my uncle's house, I shared a room with a young man by the name of Dudley Danby who, quite clearly, had some sort of hush-hush job. He wanted to know if I was interested in an occupation other than digging up the remnants of Hadrian's Wall north of Carlisle, and trying to teach elementary mental arithmetic to illiterate recruits, for such were two of my tasks at that time.

A week later, I was travelling from the Carlisle Depot to the War Office in London for an interview. I faced a Major Gielgud (the actor's brother), once met on bath-day in Finchingfield, who spoke the most excellent French and revealed nothing about the nature of my future employment. "Are you keen on taking big risks?" he asked. It was clear that the prospective job was in Occupied France. Luckily, he thought I was far too young. "This war's going to last a long time," said the major. "I'll send for you in a year." In the meantime I was to be trained in counter-intelligence, after which I would be shipped to Syria to work against the Vichy French.

In the Intelligence Corps Depot at Winchester a stupendous variety of people could be found from Scottish lairds
who owned vast *estancias* in Argentina to Cypriot waiters from
Soho. Knowledge of a second language was the prime require-
ment, and the Commandant of the Depot was reputed to have
said, "When I see on a man's papers that he's bilingual, then I
know he can't speak English."

The most exotic recruit of my contingent was an enormously
tall Finn, so fair that his colouring verged on the albino. He
had worked out his future with precision: he wanted first to be
commissioned in the Sudan Camel Corps, and after that he would
go in for undercover work. When I pointed out to him that on
both counts he was a loser – certain to be felled by the African
sun and instantly identifiable as a non-Arab – he answered gently,
"But nothing in life is easy."

It was essential to mould these disparate individuals into a
coherent unit. In the ways of all armies, it was deemed that
only when their spirit had been flattened out would it be
possible to build up an *esprit-de-corps*. To that effect the Depot
was staffed with officers and N.C.O.s drawn from the Guards
Regiments. The Potsdam-like discipline would have pleased the
great Frederick himself.

Every morning at inspection time Major Rankin, who was only
slightly less tall than the Finn, moved majestically through the
open ranks of fours. Hyperactive sergeants and corporals dashed
around, looking for infractions. The scene was reminiscent of an
aircraft-carrier and its escort of destroyers frantically searching for
a hostile sub. We were minutely inspected, from the rear of our
cap-badges to the instep of our boots; like their exposed and visible
parts, both had to exhibit a high polish. Barks from the N.C.O.s
exploded constantly. "Get yer 'air cut!" was the most frequent. "I
saw yer talkin' in the ranks!" was the most taunting, because the
moment you said, "No, Sir!" then you had been talking in the ranks
and you were on a charge. A year later I would be grateful for the
control we acquired on these morning inspections.

In spite of its spit-and-polish and its craziness, I enjoyed
Winchester, for the friends I made there, mostly; but also for the
motorcycle riding, unarmed combat, pistol shooting, long marches
and excellent food – all things pleasurable for a young man just

out of his teens. I don't know precisely how many failed the course, but it must have been close to half. They were returned to their regiments.

The serious counter-intelligence work took place at Matlock, a spa in Derbyshire that had been completely taken over by the Corps. The security was strict, and the discipline was lax. Many of the staff were attractive girls in uniform trained to report any student who tried to impress them at night with the information he had received during the day. The culprit would instantly be transferred back to his regiment. As note-taking was not allowed, we used to go over the lectures while walking in the company of a friend. Whether it was true or merely designed to frighten us, we had been warned that the pubs and tea-houses of the region were staffed with I.C. personnel, and we had better keep our mouths shut if we didn't want to be reported. I don't think, however, that Admiral Canaris, head of the Abwehr, the German secret services, would have given an old bratwurst to know what was going on at Matlock. The only titillating piece of information I ever heard I'm convinced was pure invention. A week before the German invasion was due, the story went, all over Britain chalked signs appeared on walls, fences, doors and lamp-posts; they were the work of agents operating in our midst, and they indicated here a communist, here a Jew, here a collaborating fascist, to facilitate the work of the incoming Gestapo operatives.

When training was over, a number of people, some in uniform, others in mufti, came to interview the graduates. They were all leading mysterious lives, about which they were secretive, but which they proposed to share with us. I met and was questioned by several of them, and alas turned down the one who seemed keenest to have me join his organisation and whom I found most *sympathique*. His job was screening French refugees to try and ferret out any German agent infiltrated among them. The prospect of undergoing sequential and ignominious periods of basic training with the Free French held no appeal. But the proposition wasn't all that it seemed: some months later, coming out of Claridge's I ran into one of my Matlock chums who had said yes to the offer. He was wearing civilian dress and it certainly didn't look as if he was spending much time square-bashing with pig farmers from Brittany. I never learned the true nature of his work.

I was eventually informed that as the officer establishment for the Intelligence Corps was filled up in England, I was to go to Cairo and there be commissioned as a second lieutenant. Major Gielgud's promise was about to be fulfilled. Until it was time to leave, however, I was to carry secret despatches from Winchester to Oxford and back. These summer days of '41 were often to be recalled later in the Thai and Burmese jungle: almost daily, I rode my Triumph motorbike along twisty, leafy lanes, had lunch in Oxford, and was back in Winchester for drinks before dinner, or a walk at sunset around the cathedral with its doors painted fire red.

The weeks went by and I thought I had been forgotten. I complained about being idle. Consequently I was posted, with the rank of corporal, to a Field Security Unit. This meant that I could now look forward to a life of unparalleled tediousness, at home or abroad, of checking civilian passes, inspecting the contents of ships' holds and tracing imbecilic rumours to their source. My impatience, in other words, had "blown it".

The 15th Field Security Section was attached to the 18th Division. Largely made up of East Anglian regiments, it was then standing by to go to Iran; its men were not considered first-line shock troops, and the division's duty was essentially to protect lines of communication.

As befitted wearers of the I.C. badge on their forage caps, my new companions were a mixed group. The Commanding Officer was a rotund captain, ex-Cairo police, who, malicious tongues would have it, had been inspector of brothels. His batman was the only private among us. His name was Bussey and he had been a London bus driver. Of the eleven N.C.O.s, the most senior was our sergeant-major, a regular soldier and a kindly old sweat; among the others, you could find a professional iceskater; a man who tended War Graves in Bethune, France; a car salesman who ate nothing but eggs and bacon which he claimed were a complete food; a devout Scottish schoolteacher; and Louis, a diminutive Frenchman whose basic English owed a great debt to Chicago gangster movies.

I was told to establish myself in a village on the Norfolk coast: from there I would be responsible for the area's security.

The local curate billeted me. In the most tactful way, he also tried to convert me to Christianity while I tried to convert his daughter to other and less saintly activities. Neither the curate nor I met any success. From the vicarage I "liaised" daily with the chief of police, the station master and the publican in order to find out if any suspicious character had been lurking around. A flutter of interest entered my life on the day I was advised that two German agents had been landed on the Norfolk coast by U-Boat. Later we heard that one of them had promptly been caught. Every piece of clothing, every object in his suitcase, was of impeccable British origin with the exception of a German sausage, the like of which had not been seen in Britain for two years. The *wurst* was to tide him over the first twenty-four hours after landing. Alas for him, it also tied a knot around his neck. He was duly hanged, along with his companion.

I have been unable to find a precise reference to these two unfortunates in post-war records. However, I'll let the story stand as a small personal myth with which to adorn my career as a spycatcher.

THREE

On October 29, 1941, we walked up the gangplank of the
Duchess of Atholl tied up in the Greenock docks. The sight of the
dirty, streaky-sided steamer and the feel of the Scottish rain made
the prospect of our posting in Persia, via Basra, our immediate
destination at the northern tip of the Persian Gulf, appear like a
holiday in the sun. No one, after all, was killing anyone else in Iraq
or in Iran. We were allotted three cabins, an enormous privilege
when we saw how everyone else, N.C.O.s and men that is, was
jammed prone in airless, sweaty holds. For myself I don't remember
anything more traumatic on that trip than the twice-daily meetings
with cockroaches in the stew – the only food served during the ten
days we were on board.

Five days out, the convoy was nowhere near the Straits of
Gibraltar but halfway to Halifax, Nova Scotia. On that windswept,
sunny morning, a large fleet appeared over the horizon. We soon
found ourselves encased inside an American task force. Planes took
off from the carrier and dropped messages of welcome on the
troopships. Signals broke out on the masts of the cruiser and the
destroyers. Greetings were bellowed on the loud-hailers, and the
air vibrated with the deep voices of the ships' horns. All this was
not only comforting (so far our escort had consisted of one cruiser,
H.M.S. *Calypso*, and two four-stack First World War destroyers
of Lend-Lease origin), but surprising; the United States at the
time was not a belligerent. The American escort was the result of
a private arrangement between Roosevelt and Churchill.

In Halifax, the 18th Division transferred to U.S. Coast Guard
transports which included the ex-SS *America, Manhattan* and
Washington, the latter renamed the U.S.S. *Mount Vernon,* and

our home for the next two and a half months. No one was allowed ashore except the Field Security sleuths whose job was to find out how much the local population knew or cared about American involvement in a foreign war. I thought I'd carry out my first investigation in a drugstore, over a cup of coffee. The abundance of goods and food displayed was so bewildering that all I could ask for was a banana: like German sausages they had disappeared from the United Kingdom. The teenage girl behind the counter didn't show any surprise, but answered pertly, "Yes, we have no bananas, but there's a dance in town tonight." Too much was happening. I wasn't up to it. Out of my depth, I failed to rise to the invitation, and I went looking for bananas elsewhere.

As the Mediterranean was closed off by U-Boats, we could only reach the Middle East by a roundabout way. We sailed south, still with our splendid escort (under the command of Admiral Kinkaid, it later became the U.S. 7th Fleet), down the East Coast of the United States, to Trinidad where we refuelled and took on water. On the *Mount Vernon* we had been shown the bunks we would occupy eight hours out of twenty-four. Sleep was in shifts. Furthermore, the bunks were installed in what used to be the swimming-pool: at the deep end they must have been stacked ten high. We pointed out who we were and in no time we were taken to luxurious quarters, three men to a cabin. If we wanted to impress anyone we never mentioned the humdrum "Field Security". The emphasis was always on "*Intelligence* Corps".

In order to soften the likely scandal if the American public ever got news of the breach of neutrality going on in the South Atlantic, every day on the *Mount Vernon* the British paymaster met his American counterpart. Payment in gold bullion was handed over as payment for the transport of British troops; if the ship was torpedoed, each paymaster would then be responsible for his pile. It was only on December 7, 1941, Pearl Harbor day, that the operation became legitimate.

The convoy was making for Cape Town, but with a pack of German submarines lying in wait for us we were forced to make an unwelcome cruise in the vicinity of the Polar Circle. Unwelcome because we had by then been issued with our tropical kit, and our winter clothing had been stowed in the hold. The kit itself went straight back to Kipling days: only spine protectors had been discarded (they were described to us as flat, narrow pads that hung from the back of the neck down to the coccyx). The power of the Indian sun was held to be fatal: to be hatless, nay to be topeeless in the open for as little as a minute was a death warrant. These topees were monstrous objects, fragile, impossible to store, and always in the way. Flannel belly-belts, another piece of Victoriana, saved you from cholera, and the vast, floppy shorts ensured good ventilation.

Distractions on this long voyage were few. The American food was splendid and the waste abysmal. The British rank-and-file never ceased complaining. They pined for stew and bully-beef. Asparagus, courgettes and fruit went straight into the swill buckets. "Who do they think we are? Fucking rabbits?" they asked angrily. We played cards, we spent hours observing dolphins and flying-fish. Until you got to know the sights, it was entertaining to watch the tattoo show at shower time on deck. The prize, in any contest, would have gone to the sergeant who had a full foxhunt running down his back: the fox itself had gone to earth. Its only visible appendage was its brush sticking out of the sergeant's arse. The second prize was for literature rather than art: inscribed on a smooth belly, and above generous private parts was the caption "Good girls feed here."

After three happy days in Cape Town, we resumed our journey along the East Coast of Africa. The Field Security boys had already been told the news that the rest of the passengers of the U.S.S. *Mount Vernon* only heard on Christmas Day when the ship sailed through the Mombasa channel: the 53rd Brigade, with which we were travelling on the *Mount Vernon*, was being diverted to Singapore while the rest of the 18th Division was bound for Bombay where it would await orders. It very much looked as if we were about to be turned into a "gallant gesture". We couldn't know that London had given up all hope of saving Malaya. The Australians, however, were becoming very edgy, and proof had to be given that Whitehall cared. (No sooner had they reached Bombay than the other two brigades of 18th Division were ordered to turn around and steam as fast as they could to Singapore).

In Mombasa, the troops crowded into the rush huts where fat black girls gyrated sleepily to the sound of a hand-cranked gramophone. At the end of the performance the men quietly formed a line as the girls fell on their backs, legs opened, to service the customers. Louis and I went to a pleasant hotel at the edge of town. At the bar we met a Frenchman who divulged the complete plan, along with maps and diagrams, of the forthcoming invasion of Madagascar by the Free French. Over a brochette of roast goat in the bazaar we discussed whether we would report the Frenchman for breach of security. We liked him, and although we felt like sneaks and delators, we turned him in.

The situation in Malaya looked exceeding unhealthy. The Japanese were coming down the peninsula and nothing seemed to stop them. This was unexpected for they were fighting with terrible handicaps. In the air their pilots, we heard, were no match for ours: they all wore glasses. They were worsted in dogfights because, as is common knowledge, Orientals have a faulty sense of balance. On the ground, Japanese riflemen were not to be feared: they had trouble closing one eye when they took aim. And at sea, they simply copied our naval designs. Everyone knew the story of the falsified battleship plans the Americans had slipped to one of their agents: when the ship, built in a Japanese yard, came down the slip and hit the water, it flopped on its side and turned keel up!

In our little group no one was desperately eager to tackle spies and Fifth Columnists, about whom we knew nothing. We had been trained for the Middle East and its problems; we spoke the local languages – French, Italian and a little Arabic. We would be utterly wasted in the Far East. Why not disembark in Mombasa and make our way overland to where we could be useful? Our Captain agreed and approached General Beckwith-Smith who commanded the 18th Division. Permission to leave the ship was given but there was a hitch. Our captain who was returning to Cairo and its social life, had brought his dinner jacket which, along with the rest of his kit, was to be found in a trunk stored in the hold. There was no question, naturally, of unloading the hold to get at the kit. "In that case," our C.O. was reputed to have said, "we'll all go to Singapore, retrieve the trunk and make our way back to the Middle East."

We steamed full speed and without an escort across the Indian Ocean; for a day we anchored off the Maldive Islands; we dropped depth charges on putative subs, and zigzagged to the Sunda Straits between Java and Sumatra, past Krakatoa where we were joined by a Dutch cruiser and attacked by twenty-seven Japanese bombers. Finally on January 13, 1942, we docked at Singapore. A blessed heavy tropical rain hid us from aerial attack. The 15th Field Security Unit, Intelligence Corps, its captain and his dinner jacket, were now in the trap. But that was merely a passing thought, because, at last, we were ashore after two and a half months at sea. Nothing, we said, will ever be worse than what we've just been through.

Whereas 53rd Brigade was shipped off immediately to the fighting line – frighteningly close in Johore – we were driven to the village of Bukit Timah north-west of Singapore town. There, in spite of the war we were able to enjoy, for the first and last time, the privileges of being a white man, a *tuan*, in Malay. We seemed to be surrounded by servants who washed, polished, tidied, cooked, ironed, brought us iced drinks and hot water, and even shaved us while we were still in bed. I was taught how to ride a rickshaw: foot on the puller's appropriate shoulder to indicate whether to turn right or left; and feet on both shoulders to stop. While my rickshaw *wallah* was snaking through bomb craters and ruined houses I got a very distinct feeling: none of this could last very long.

Of all the new and exotic sights, nothing pleased me more than the *kampongs*, the villages inhabited by Chinese or Malays. In the course of the next years, more than any recollection of Normandy or East Anglia, they were the evocation of "home" with its secret and intimate qualities. The daytime smell of woodsmoke, and the intoxicating night scent of the frangipani, the fleeting sight of a girl at work, the sound of the drums and of the Chinese flute, a small child leading a buffalo – all these impressions struck a note which was instantly precious.

Our motorcycles were unloaded. The Captain made a deal with Headquarters Malaya Command: in exchange for our motorbikes he would be allowed to send a signal back to Intelligence Corps H.Q. in England asking permission to "proceed" to the Middle East. The answer came back too late: Go If You Can.

We read files. We were briefed about the nature of the local Fifth Column. We tried to locate the origin of anti-British broadcasts that came from within Singapore Island: we couldn't understand where the power came from, for even when we gave orders for the current to be systematically cut in different sections of the Island, the broadcasting never ceased. (An underwater cable, we learned after the war, ran under the Straits from the mainland to a rubber plantation on Singapore Island.) We investigated suspects, followed false trails, went up into Johore, retreated with the troops, were shot at by snipers, cowered under shelling, and got caught in monstrous traffic jams of military vehicles while the Japs were racing through the jungle carrying their bicycles on their shoulders.

The British, Australian and Indian divisions came down the Malay Peninsula in an ever more impetuous rush as they were outflanked, outfought and leapfrogged by the Japanese. For us, late arrivals, the overseas campaign was drastically abbreviated: two weeks only after we'd come down the gangplank of the *Mount Vernon*, the Causeway linking Singapore Island with the mainland was blown up by British sappers. We were now bottled up, along with refugees in their tens of thousands, and it was the Imperial Japanese Army who held the cork.

The signs were bad: the *Prince of Wales* and the *Repulse* had been sunk by bespectacled pilots with a faulty sense of balance; the last ship had left Singapore with women and children, the last Hurricanes had been shot out of the sky; and the huge guns at the Naval Base couldn't be turned around to blast the rubbershod Japanese out of the jungle. The worst was to be feared.

On February 8, the first detachments of the I.J.A.'s Guards Division landed in the mangrove swamps on the north-east coast of the island. Caught in the frantic disorganisation of the last few days, almost every member of the Field Security was now operating independently. How or why, I can't remember, but I found myself under the orders of Lieutenant Colonel Hutchinson, the intelligence head of 53rd Brigade, known in military parlance as G-I.

The night of the landings, for the first time in forty-eight hours, I lay down in a tent at Brigade H.Q. Poleaxed with fatigue, not even bothering to extract my 32-calibre Smith & Wesson from its thigh holster, I fell into a deep sleep. Before midnight, the Colonel's batman shook me awake.

"The Japs have landed here, opposite the Australians," said G-I, pointing at map coordinates. "And here, the Norfolks have caught a Malay. They think he's a Fifth Columnist. Get on your bike and find out. And do whatever you have to." Meaning, shoot him.

On that night ride thoughts arose half-formed through a slough of fatigue, and vanished into unconsciousness. Exhaustion brought about hallucinations that altered perception and twisted judgment, and when the road came under shelling, I didn't stop and take cover.

What happened to the Malay I never found out, and it was weeks later that I learned what took place during that last and obliterated part of the night ride: obliterated because in spite of the shelling, and still on my bike, I must have fallen asleep.

Two men on guard at a roadblock opened fire as chance took me right through the small gap left open for pedestrians. In the darkness, they failed to hit me. Or to wake me. At a second roadblock, the lieutenant and the sergeant who had been warned of my arrival described how they saw a motorcycle slam against the tangle of barbed wire and tree trunks (memory: the whip-zoom image of a tree smashing into my face), and the rider, who took off like a stuntman, vaulting and crashing on the opposite side. The lieutenant shone a flashlight on the débris. It was not unfamiliar; we had known each other on the Stock Exchange.

Three days later, I regained consciousness in Selarang Military Hospital. All traces of the immediate past had been wiped out. Disparate events floated up from the darkness like dream fragments. At first in discrete blobs, but with neurons reconnecting, the web of memory began again to spread backwards.

That afternoon, the hospital was half destroyed in an air raid, and the survivors were hastily loaded into a string of ambulances. Zero fighters swooped down and strafed the convoy. On the third pass, the roof of the ambulance in which I lay with five others was ripped open, killing the driver and his mate. By evening, however, I was stretched out on the floor, in a corridor of the Civil and General Hospital.

Like an antiphon, a continuous murmur overlaid the moans and the delirium of the wounded. Mephitic and pervasive, it swept through the hospital's wards, corridors and landings.

"What the fuck d'you think is going on?"

"Fuck if I know. Nips packing in, if you ask me."

"We're packing in, more bloody likely."

"What d'you think the bastards'll do to us?"

"Finish us off, I reckon."

"Fuckin' 'ell!"

"Holy Mother of God!"

Through the small window left open in my bandaged head all I saw was the blur of the ceiling and a fuzzy light fixture. But like everyone else in Singapore, on that afternoon of February 15, I was trying to decode the sounds of field artillery, small arms fire and aerial bombing.

The gunfire – theirs and ours – was certainly dying down. Even the dry, metallic rat-tat-tat of the Mambus, the Japanese equivalent of our Bren guns, was intermittent.

Strangest of all, apart from reconnaissance flights, there'd hardly been any air activity all day. Except for a frightening low-level attack on two Bofors anti-aircraft guns sited right in the hospital grounds. "Can't blame the Nips for that, can you?" said a private from the Argylls, quietly and reasonably.

At dusk the sound of gunfire ceased altogether. So did the wounded's speculations.

Later, carrying a flashlight (the electric power had been cut off, and the fuel for the emergency generator had run out), a medical officer came into the corridor where I was lying on a stretcher. "I've got bad news, boys. We've surrendered." Men were sobbing in the dark.

The throb in my head and the blood clotting my nose and throat buffered the subtler delineations of feeling. I sensed only a nameless dread. An inner voice, however, said "Don't anticipate. Submit. Trust. There's nothing you can do."

Like scum rising above dark waters, disbelief rose through the dread. These events simply didn't fit in the pattern of my life. Ahead was the unknown. And the unknowable. For the first time I felt entirely alone.

The senior British doctor, three Japanese officers and a civilian interpreter came through the wards shortly after dawn. I could hear the long swords rattle and clang as they hit the cavalry boots. I turned my head and forced myself to look. The Japanese were smaller than I thought they would be. Two of them wore eye glasses and the interpreter had a stiff brush moustache, just like the caricatures. But they didn't in the least behave like caricatures:

their uniforms were immaculate, and they carried themselves with the calm of the victors.

Orders were given: by 11 a.m. the hospital had to be vacated to allow Japanese wounded to take our place.

Once more I was lifted on to a stretcher and loaded into an ambulance. After halts and challenges from Japanese patrols we reached the Singapore waterfront with its tall office buildings. I was deposited on a desk, and wedged between two typewriters so that I wouldn't fall off.

The battle was over, and we were not going to be massacred. The relief was indescribably sweet.

The survivors' euphoria didn't last long. It was merely the first of the four classic stages in the P.O.W.'s mental evolution.

By the time I was settled in my new territory bordered by its two Remington typewriters, Phase Two was under way. It manifested itself as an irrepressible anger directed at those responsible for our plight. Like a collective mania, it swept over everyone, regardless of rank, providing a subject of discussion to which all could contribute incontrovertible evidence; and from evidence to expertise was an easy step. Furthermore, wallowing in the emotional climate of Phase Two also produced a valuable side effect: it exonerated acts of cowardice, and it justified remission of duty.

It was of course painfully obvious that our leaders at Fort Canning, the headquarters of Malaya Command, had shown neither military skill nor leadership. The defence of the peninsula turned into a dismal rout. Anyone who, at company strength, found himself obliged to retreat in classic First World War style because a squad of Japanese infantry was reported in the rear, felt entitled to speak of the folly of his superior officers with the authority of a lecturer at the Staff College. But if those above were held in universal contempt and loathing, it was also profitable to blame the British if you were Australian, the Australians if you were British, while everyone came down hard on the Indians. As for the Indians, who, from the start of captivity had been segregated from the British and the Australians, it's not hard to guess whom they blamed.

Phase Three, which came much later, brought resignation.

Not that of the sage, but the passivity of the hungry, and the inaction brought about by hopelessness. It was in Phase Three that the vast majority settled until the end of their imprisonment.

The fourth and last stage – an obsession with escape – rarely occured in Japanese P.O.W. camps for two understandable reasons. The first was that in order to reach friendly territory you had the option of a sea journey by small boat, or a land trek through jungle, both of approximately the same distance – 2,000 miles. The second was that recapture was followed by decapitation or the firing squad.

By the end of February, I was declared fit enough to join the vast mass of prisoners that had been driven into Changi, the eastern tip of Singapore Island which had been turned into a vast P.O.W. camp. The two main features of the area were the civil jail and the Army barracks. Over sixty thousand men settled into an area that was designed to accomodate around one tenth that number.

I found the Field Security Section installed in a ground floor room of the barracks. No one had been killed, but our captain and four N.C.O.s were missing: they had escaped before capitulation. From H.Q. Malaya Command orders had been issued for so-called key personnel to leave in a final *sauve-qui-peut*. The information they possessed, so the argument ran, was to be used for the continuation of the struggle against Japan. To my surprise (for why would anyone think I was an experienced Japanese spycatcher?), it appeared that my name had been on the list of those detailed to escape. I was tracked down to the Selarang Hospital where it was learned that I'd been evacuated on the very last ship to leave Singapore Harbour. Lucky bugger, my companions of 15th Field Security who stayed behind must have thought.

The unexpected reversal of my fate might have been one of the reasons for their kindness when I showed up without any gear or clothes except for what I was wearing, and unencumbered by any object except for a watch, a toothbrush and a piece of soap. Yet by the end of my first day in Changi I could be said to possess the basic necessities of life. The main offering was a vast wicker armchair which in combination with a crate was to be my bed.

It took me two days to rid it of bedbugs. I still loathe the bloodsuckers above all other forms of pests: I've had rats run over me in Kashmir; fleas feast on me in Tibet; and in New

York, I found cockroaches copulating in my toothglass. Nothing, however, is quite as revolting as bedbugs.

The internal administration of the camps was left to the prisoners. The Japanese didn't want to immobilize more personnel that was absolutely necessary for this ignominious duty, and many of the guards were Koreans. In their wish to appear more Catholic than the Pope, these Korean auxiliaries were harsher than the Japanese themselves. They had been given Japanese names but British Lee-Enfield rifles. The reason was that on the butt of the standard Japanese rifle could be found a small brass disc which carried the image of the Imperial Chrysanthemum. Only a true descendant of Amaterasu, the Sun Goddess who struck the ocean with her wand and created the islands of Japan from the droplets that scattered, was held worthy of such a trust. Adding to his vexations, a Korean's pay was well below that of his Japanese equivalent; and as it was difficult for him ever to reach even non-commissioned rank, almost any Japanese was entitled to slap his face. From his dismal position at the bottom of the ladder he joyfully discovered that there was an even lower rung, a basement rung as it were. Precariously perched on it, was a white prisoner-of-war.

We all knew and practised the low bow, hands held along the thighs, whenever we saw any of our captors. Martin McCall, a friend who had served in the legal service of the Federated Malay States, once had to draw aside to make way for a party of Japanese staff officers who were on an inspection tour of the camp. He bowed deeply, eyes down, holding his breath. These were not, you understand, common jailers who rated a perfunctory bow. No one in the group bothered to acknowledge the obeisance except for a captain who turned and addressed Martin in fluent English. "How pleasant to meet you again," he said "I do hope your health is good." The captain had been Martin's barber in Kuala Lumpur. Interestingly, he had never allowed his Pidgin English vocabulary to exceed the strict needs of his trade.

My own first contact with a Japanese officer left me with a feeling of rancour. I had been asked, one evening, to "take" roll-call – to be the N.C.O. responsible for parading and numbering a small group of men, no larger than platoon strength. The I.J.A. representative on this occasion was a young subaltern who spoke

English, which he filtered through a handkerchief held under his nose. I asked him if he had a cold. "*Baka!*" he answered. "Idiot! You smell. You smell very bad." It's well known that you can tell someone he's a cretinous fool and he might forgive you. But you can't accuse a person of being smelly. The insult reaches a primitive and enduring core of feeling. I had heard of *fetor judaicus*, one of the more imaginative inventions found in the Protocol of the Elders of Zion, but I suspected that the subaltern's disgust was not directed at me personally. Still, as I've said, I was filled with rancour.

More than a month went by before I came across the lieutenant again. Now, however, he had the use of both his hands: he wasn't holding his handkerchief under his nose. I asked him if he had got used to our smell. "I have not," he answered, "now you smell OK. You eat no meat since you become pu-ri-so-na."

Food was the pivotal aspect of our lives, the source of our inventiveness, the subject of most conversation, and the recurring content of dreams. We evoked the sensuous enjoyment of bread, cheese and pickles with the same longing tones we used to describe a quail resting on a canapé of *foie gras*. We kicked ourselves for the second helpings we'd turned away. We planned orgiastic menus to be consumed after liberation. The lack of food was the mainspring for the black market, with its huge risks: bashings, kickings and slappings; at worst, solitary confinement and special treatment organised by the Kempeitai, the Military Gendarmerie-cum-Gestapo whose reputation for ferocity matched the inventiveness of their tortures.

The first month in Changi was the worst. The brutal change of diet caused unpleasant and contradictory symptoms. Constipation could last weeks for some, while diarrhoea forced others to settle close to the latrines. Although the main staple, in fact almost the only food we received, was rice, it couldn't be said to be without variety. At times it was mere sweepings – broken grains, husk and gravel; for a while it came dyed yellow and stank of sulphur; or it might shelter a variety of insect life: depending on the shipment, weevils or fat white maggots would be the main inhabitants.

Louis, the Frenchman with the Chicago mobster accent, was our business head, banker and provider. His generosity was as great as his ingenuity, which in turn was as keen as his nose for money. Most days he was off travelling through the camp, meeting his suppliers, collecting watches and fountain-pens, keeping assignations with Korean guards, trading his wares for food and tobacco, returning to see his clients and delivering the promised goods. I gave him my Jaeger-LeCoultre watch to sell but it didn't carry a name much in repute among the guards. Rolex for watches and Parker for pens were the brand names in demand. In exchange for my watch I got a tin of Colman's mustard, a head of garlic and a pack of Chinese cigarettes. Definitely not durable goods. The mustard and the garlic, however, were ideal accompaniments to help the rice go down.

It was only when the first Dutch P.O.W.s arrived from Java that the food improved. A high proportion were of mixed blood. They taught us how to cook rice and how to use *blachang*, our main source of protein. Blachang was the Malay fisherman's equivalent of the English Patum Peperium or Gentleman's Relish, a powerfully fishy and traditional paste. *Blachang* was made by spreading out in the sun the remains of inedible fish, sprinkling them with sea salt and letting them rot into a soft and putrid mass. British P.O.W. cuisine used it for turning out fish cakes, merely adding the stuff in its raw state to soggy rice balls. The Javanese recipe was to fry the blachang in palm oil, hot chillies and garlic (bought on the black market and later at the canteen set up by the Japanese), and to add it in small amounts to boiled rice; the mixture was then pushed into a short length of bamboo sealed at both ends with a mud plug, and baked under hot coals. With such skills, the Dutch and their East Indian cooks were the first prisoners to make money from "manufacturing" rather than by trading on the black market.

At the time of the move to Changi, we had been ordered to hand over any radios we found in the old barracks. We had a number we hid after dismantling them, but the most powerful set was installed intact by James Mudie, a resourceful and courageous B.B.C. engineer, in the festering underground chamber of a wrecked twin 6-inch gun turret on Changi Point. The Japanese were unlikely to poke their noses in such an insalubrious place.

Possession of a radio was punishable by death. It was a crime worse than escape. The news heard daily on the set was therefore disseminated to relatively few people in camp – among whom was the Intelligence Corps section to which I belonged.

It was clear that that the war was going against us. The Japanese were masters of the Pacific from Hawaii to Australia. The Germans had overrun European Russia and were about to roll up Egypt. But for the sixty thousand men in Changi the war situation was encapsulated in three words: Home By Christmas.

The rumours making the rounds of Changi were indeed encouraging: the Allies had landed in France; the Germans were in full rout, pushed out of Russia, North Africa and Italy; and the Russians were in sight of the Berlin suburbs. Curiously, however, the Imperial Japanese forces were never mentioned (although, even at that early date, their naval forces earmarked for the invasion of Australia had suffered a crucial defeat). The reason was clear: the Japanese P.O.W. Camp Administration was the source of the rumours. Its purpose, we imagined, was to demoralise the prisoners by building up their hopes, and letting them down when eventually they leaked out the true situation. The equation was evident; the lower the morale, the fewer the guards.

We in the know had no illusions. We also thought there was little hope of surviving the many years that clearly would be needed to overcome the Axis powers.

One night I dreamed I would be a prisoner for three and a half years. The dream hit me with the force of prediction. It was singular in two aspects: both for its acuity and its persistence in my memory. When you were free of fever, dreams were generally pleasurable. They recalled the inaccessible – food, sex or family. But this particular dream was neither pleasant nor threatening. Its flatness was its strength.

If I took it at face value, if I believed in its sybilline contents, then come what may I would survive imprisonment. However I couldn't accept it in that form: the stuff of the dream, I felt, pointed to probabilities rather than certainties. It presented itself as a pattern rather than as a fixed design. The odds, in other words, were on the side of life rather than death.

I understood that prefigured ends are not unalterable; that they can be self-fulfilling or they can be changed. In this case, quite clearly, it was in my hands to try and shape my future and make it fit the dream's promise.

FOUR

Three and a half years, if I believed the dream, was a long time to spend in Japanese hands, and I seriously set about finding the kind of skill that would increase the odds on my survival.

I knew there was a drastic shortage of Japanese speakers, although this wasn't obvious within the confines of Changi, a huge area, because encounters with the guards were relatively infrequent.

At our own prisoner headquarters (still labelled without a hint of derision "Headquarters Malaya Command") half a dozen interpreters were always on hand. But in the outlying areas the problem was clearly visible on the few occasions when I left Changi with working parties. At the root of most "bashings" was the inability to communicate with the Japanese. Whenever a prisoner broke the rules and was caught, if he was unable to defend himself, or admit that he was in the wrong (generally the wisest course), both he and the Japanese were locked in a situation from which one-sided violence was the only possible outcome.

Groups of prisoners were constantly being sent away to unknown destinations. Without interpreters they were sure to face grave difficulties.

It seemed that I'd found one answer to the problem of acquiring a skill: it was simply to learn the language. A Japanese speaker was bound to be in demand, and his value would be such that he wouldn't be easily expendable.

Acquiring the knowledge wouldn't be a problem as Malay primers designed to teach Japanese, or *Nippon-go*, to the local population, soon appeared for sale. Their aim was to promote the linguistic unity of the "Greater East Asia Co-Prosperity Sphere" which was meant to replace the British Imperial presence. (The best graffiti to appear on the walls of Syonan-to – "City of the South" – as Singapore had been renamed, read Nippon Come, Nippon Go.) As we had all quickly picked up elementary "kitchen" Malay – to Rajah Malay what pidgin is to English – I started my studies with these books until I could replace them with more elaborate English-Japanese grammars. It was hard going.

Someone must have mentioned my fumbling efforts to Colonel Hutchinson. It might have been our Sergeant Major who reported to him regularly. We had switched from our original counter-espionage functions to "espionage" pure and simple. The reason was that, for a time, it was thought possible that a number of amputees might be repatriated. It became our task to sit from dawn to dusk on Changi Hill, from where the harbour was visible, and note down all movement of shipping, a description of each vessel and its approximate tonnage. The amputees were to memorise this information, the hope being that months later they would regurgitate it with profit to our naval authorities. The idea was ludicrous, but we didn't criticise it: the view from the hill was beautiful, and reading a book in the shade of the palm trees, by a flowering hibiscus, was certainly a more pleasant way of spending the day than shovelling rubble in Syonan-to.

Hutch wanted to know if I would devote myself exclusively to the study of Japanese. If so, I would be taken off all other duties; lessons would be arranged with one of the official British interpreters. Lastly, money would be found for grammars, notebooks, and other supplies I might need.

Daily I took a long walk to H.Q. Malaya Command. Gerard Rawlings, a missionary's son who had been brought up in Japan, became my teacher, my first *sensei*. Rawlings warned me of the enormous difficulties ahead, and prophesised that by the time I was able to speak the language I was also likely to have a breakdown. He was right: six months later, I fell into a depression, couldn't remember the most elementary Japanese words, and nightmares disturbed my sleep. I was removed to the P.O.W. hospital, given vitamins, and shielded from the sight of guards. After forty-eight hours I was sane again.

My second *sensei* was Captain (Padre) Andrews, an old Scot who had been in a parish in a remote part of Japan. Of all the interpreters who had been born and brought up in that country, he was the least in awe of the Japanese. His devotion to drink gave him, he believed, a special insight into Bushido, the doctrine that animated the Japanese Armed Forces. "The spirit of Bushido," he used to say to anyone who questioned him on the subject, "is generally found in a well corked bottle." Yet of all the Japanese speakers he was probably the most skilful linguist, and the one who knew best the simple folk of Japan. From him, there was more to learn about the country and its meaning than from anyone else.

On the Japanese side, the senior interpreter was an aristocratic-looking lieutenant of samurai background whose kindness and generosity were known throughout the camp. He always came to see me with small presents, and encouraged me in my studies. He provided drawing materials for Ronald Searle who was assiduously (and illegally) recording scenes of P.O.W. life. Requesting these materials was a risk, yet I felt certain of the lieutenant's discretion: he would never ask to see Searle's work. In veiled words, he would let us know that he felt much sympathy for what we were going through, and simplistically, we believed that he "saw things as we did"; that, deep down, he was on our side. The reality was far more complex: after hearing the Imperial Rescript announcing unconditional surrender in August 1945, he was the first officer in Singapore to blow his brains out.

His colleague, Koryasu San, a quiet civilian who wished to appear penetrated by military ardour, and therefore thought it proper to look gruff in our presence, loved Beethoven quartets and Jane Austen. The pocket of his tunic was always bulging with one of her novels. He thought of her as an English Lady Murasaki.

The camp was visited by all manner of Japanese dignitaries, including some scientists who came to see our home-grown industries. The vitamin B "factory" attracted most attention. Peanuts had become available but they proved too much of a strain for our weakened digestive systems. A biochemist among us thought of a way to break down their coarse internal structure by means of a fermentation process using the sharp and tough mould of rice. The really profitable spin-off was that the fermentation produced a substantial quantity of vitamin B. The end product wasn't pleasant to chew but it cleared my first bout of neuritic beri-beri.

The most unexpected visitor was Foujita, a Japanese expatriate who was as much at home in Montparnasse as any Paris-born painter. To find him in Changi was exceedingly unlikely. Hubert, my childhood friend in Paris (we were three when we met because our nannies were inseparable), had studied painting with Marie Laurencin who of course knew Foujita. With that pretext, I went to see him. He was wearing a strange paramilitary uniform. We spoke French and he was delighted. "*Mon pauvre ami,*" he said, "*je ne vous demande pas ce que vous faîtes ici. . .*" But I wanted to know the how and the why of his presence in Singapore. "I would have been perfectly happy to stay in Paris," he said, "But when Japan got into the war, *ces messieurs* in Tokyo requested the Germans to ship me back. You can imagine what kind of journey I had. *Et maintenant, me voici peintre des Armées!*" Poor Foujita, what a come-down from painting smooth, delicious women, and smooth, depraved cats to Official War Artist.

By October 1942 I ceased being a mere satellite to official interpreters. I was thought proficient enough to "fly solo" in uncomplicated, set occasions. Roll call was one such daily occurrence, but what was normally a simple situation could occasionally develop into a difficult one owing to the Japanese lack of facility with figures and the prisoners' slow progress in numbering off in Nippon-go. It was said that the enormous mental effort required of Japanese children to learn the ideograms (a minimum of 3,000 is needed to read the popular press) resulted in a reduced ability with mental arithmetic. For my part, I did what I could to teach Japanese numbers to the people around me. It wasn't always a rewarding task: some of my less gifted, in fact semi-literate, students accused me behind my back of being "Jap-happy" – implying that I was halfway down the road to becoming a collaborator. Their reluctance to learn the numbers was naturally regarded as a patriotic gesture. To my friends, however, I became *Uruman san.* Uruman was the way my name had been transliterated by the guards, the sound "l" being unknown in Japanese. They always added *san*, Mister, except on those occasions when I was about to get my face slapped.

Attempting to navigate through the labyrinthine Japanese mind was, after food, everyone's favourite intellectual occupation. In this maze we could distinguish three main disconnected areas, and the problem was to discover a "unified field theory" that would make sense.

There was, first of all, their naïvety (conveniently putting aside our own credulousness, the stories we had heard and believed on the ship concerning their physical handicaps). We found it very funny to have to write down the answers to such questions as, "What were your feelings when you left England?" ("Sadness at leaving my loved ones. But pride also, for I was defending the glory of the British Empire.") Or: "What are your favourite sports?" ("Cross-country running and sailing" – perfect training for future P.O.W.s). Their own war anecdotes could well have been lifted out of a comic book about an early Nippon Superman. My favourite related the deeds of the fighter pilot whose undercarriage got shot up in an aerial fight. Rather than attempt a belly-landing, using his sword he opened two holes in the cockpit floor. This enabled him to lower his legs which, as they touched ground, became substitute wheels, thus saving the aircraft for another day and another battle. It was also mentioned that he was a champion runner.

Everyone was familiar with the second chamber of the labyrinth where hysteria often accompanied sadism. During the Malayan campaign no prisoners were taken, and their execution was carried out, on many occasions, in a gratuitously cruel manner. When the Allied forces surrendered in large numbers a wholesale massacre was impossible, and we were spared. However, some twenty thousand Chinese were murdered in the few days following the capitulation. During the ride from the Singapore waterfront to Changi, we had seen their heads stuck on bamboo poles.

Officers and senior N.C.O.s were eager to blood their swords; those below, their bayonets. Before the kill they worked themselves into an uncontrollable rage. But humans weren't the only target: outside the office building where we had been evacuated, I had seen Japanese troops dousing dogs with petrol and setting them on fire. That they had not signed the Geneva Convention was one thing. We could understand (if not appreciate) their viewpoint without accepting it – that allowing oneself to become prisoner was to abdicate honour, virtue, dignity and the right to stay alive. But using human beings for bayonet practice and torturing animals for laughs had nothing to do with these considerations.

The so-called "Selarang Incident" was a taste of how far they would go to subdue their prisoners. An order came from Major General Shimpei Fukuye, Commandant of all P.O.W. Camps in Malaya, requiring us individually to sign a form swearing that we would never attempt to escape. We refused, or rather, Lieutenant Colonel E.B. Holmes, commanding British and Australian troops in Changi, refused on our behalf. Such an act went against the King's Rules & Regulations. (Holmes had become the senior Allied officer as anyone above the rank of full colonel had been shipped off to Formosa, as Taiwan was then known.)

On September 2, Colonel Holmes and the area commanders were taken to witness the execution of four men, two British and two Australians, who had tried to escape. The firing squad was composed of Sikhs, ex-British Police or Indian Army, who had gone over to Chandra Bose's Indian National Army. I have a transcript (on the back of a Japanese roll-call form) of what took place.

Lt. Col. Okama called to the firing party and indicated on his own body the target they were to aim for. Lt. Okasaki gave the order to fire. The four men fell. Cpl. Bravington [one of the two Australians] sat up and said, 'Please shoot me through the heart. You have shot me through the arm.'

Lt. Okasaki turned to the party that had witnessed the incident and spoke to them. The interpreter translated. 'You have witnessed four men put to death. They attempted escape against Japanese orders. It is impossible to escape because the great Japanese Army covers all countries in the South, and anybody escaping must be caught. We do not like to put them to death. *You have not signed the paper saying you will not escape which is an admission that you all intend to escape.*

By six p.m. that day everyone in Changi, with the exception of 1,500 very sick men, was herded into Selarang Barracks. We numbered 15,400, and we squeezed ourselves into an area designed to hold 900. There were no latrines, no food and only two water-points. Machine-gunners surrounded us. Dysentery and malaria were prevalent when we went in, but after three days, diphtheria broke out and threatened to turn fast into an epidemic. General Fukuye then announced that unless we signed, the sick and dying that had been left in hospital would join us. We signed.

And in the third chamber of the Japanese enigma, was found a sentimentality beyond our understanding.

At the opposite pole of Lieutenant Okasaki's words was the communiqué signed "R. Fukuda, i/c No. 1 Transport Battalion. Singapore, Summer 1942". It is addressed to "The Soldiers of T.L.5" under his command, whose sickness rate was higher than other working parties.

I think [the sickness] is caused by the matter that the soldiers of T.L.5 cannot make their spirits high. . . To work for the enemies of yesterday is not cheerful, but the fact that they drive their lorries is that they can give life to themselves by their lorries. As for the repairers, when they have finished their repairing they will be in gladness, forgetting their enemies and themselves. On the way of repairing, they can expect the gratification of finishing their work.

If the soldiers of T.L.5 cannot enjoy such gladness, then I think they cannot feel life worth living. Indeed in rough beds, thinking of pleasures of past days, their own native places, wives and children, they will be shut in deep sorrow without exception. Moreover, when they catch diseases in their bodies, the darkness in their minds will increase and the disease will be serious until death.

My dear English soldiers, our lives are not short from some points of view, the days of peace will come sooner or later. If the Peace comes you can go to your dear country and work for her mankind and God. Although you are grieved, a day is 24 hours. Although you are cheerful, a day is 24 hours. If you are sad or not, the morning comes just the same. So you must raise your minds, spending your time without sadness, and thereupon you must expel your illness. There is a proverb in Nippon that 'illness comes from the mind'. The converse is true. Make your minds cheerful, drive the illness far away and keep your health in good condition until the day when you go back to your dear home.

As the year drew to a close, the cooks started hoarding rations for a blowout on Christmas Day. November 1942 was a month of famine. From the Japanese we received one cigarette per man (the precious, delicious, KOOA brand, made locally) as a *Kurisomasu presento*. Tobacco not only cut down hunger, but as solace and comforter it surpassed any nourishment. I never came across anyone who gave it up in order to increase his food purchasing power, but I met non-smokers who, in camp, took up the habit. Tobacco was readily available on the black market, dark, pungent and curly. It was known as "Sikh's Beard". Paper was far more difficult to obtain. At first the Japanese allowed us the *Syonan Times*, their local newspaper, with its imaginative accounts of heroic deeds and repeated sinkings of the whole U.S. Navy. Someone, however, must have suggested that the Emperor's portrait might find its way to the latrines, and it was banned. The most desirable rolling paper was found in Bibles. If, in the act of tearing up the Book, the user met a look of disapproval among the witnesses to the desecration, he would assure them that he always committed to memory what he called the "motto", one or two significant lines from the scrap used to roll his "ciggie".

To feed a tobacco habit it was necessary to barter whatever goods you still possessed, to trade in the black market, to supply services, or to engage in illegal or even criminal practices. True, we each received every month a tiny amount of "pay" from the Japanese. The amount depended on our rank, and on fanciful charges against it, such as rent and savings. It was vital to try and make it grow. Cooks, with access to food supplies, had an easy game; as did medical orderlies who were able to dispense special treatment.

In the way of services rendered, a pinch of Sikh's Beard would pay for your Army-issue knife to be honed to such a fine edge that you could use it to shave; a two-day supply of tobacco would pay for sandals made from old tyres as long as you contributed the scrap of rubber. It was even possible to find someone who would stand in for you if you didn't feel well enough to go out on a working party. The most exotic service was surely rendered by an old-time sergeant who removed his upper and lower dentures before performing fellatio on the few prisoners still exercised by sexual feelings.

Finally, came the problem of finding a light. As matches were nonexistent, we made our own lighters. They were ingenious, but required exceptional body co-ordination to operate them. The device consisted of three parts: a silex stone in lieu of flint; a small metal box (Oxo Cubes were the best) containing carbonised kapok for tinder; and a steel disc the size of a ten-pence coin. Two small holes had been drilled in the disc, and through them two strands of string, each about four feet long, had been threaded. The strings were tied together at both ends, with the disc riding halfway along the device. When he needed to light his cigarette, if a chair wasn't handy, the smoker had to lie on his back, hold one end of the string between his teeth, while he hooked the other around his big toe. One hand held the silex stone, and the other the tinder box. The operation consisted first in moving the string leg in a bicycle-like pumping action causing the said string to wind and unwind, which in turn imparted a rapid rotation and counter-rotation to the disc; then in getting the hand holding the stone to present it to the disc which, striking the stone, produced sparks; finally, in manoeuvring the tinder box into the stream of sparks which would then set the kapok smouldering.

It was of course simpler to go up to someone you saw smoking and ask him for a light. But unless he knew you, he would probably turn you down: a prevalent trick was to walk around with a hollow tube of paper, and surreptitiously cadge a couple of draws from the proffered cigarette.

I bring up these sweepings from remote corners of my memory to illustrate some of the problems that had to be solved. Many of the mechanical everyday gestures of the past now required unusual concentration. Operating the lighter properly, for instance, demanded the kind of attention needed when changing direction in skiing – at the same time shifting body weight, angling the steel edges of the skis and pivoting the heels. (My love of skiing was such that in the winter of '39 I had volunteered, but in vain, for the British unit that was going to Finland to fight the Russians.) Once the physical co-ordination had been acquired, using the lighter smoothly and rapidly brought about a keen sense of physical gratification.

Once a week, our turn came to borrow a hand-cranked phonograph and a few classical records. Sitting in the moist darkness we were penetrated by the transcendental joy of a Mozart piano concerto, or consoled by the languor of a slow movement in a Schubert quartet. Granados's Spanish Dance No. 5 plunged me into a slough of nostalgia: for years, as a child in Paris, I had heard that slow, hypnotic piano piece filtering down into my room from the apartment upstairs. Now I listened to it lying on my back, scanning the Equatorial sky for the Southern Cross, enervated by the cloying and intoxicating scent of the frangipani.

Being an interpreter gave me an immense advantage: I felt useful. Some thought the price too heavy. They noticed that interpreters, spending so much of their time with the Japanese, were a natural target for their blows. By interposing himself between a guard and a prisoner, the interpreter stood a good chance of being hit alongside the accused. Attempting to patch up a dispute, if he took the prisoner's side, made him an accessory to the crime. The price of failure was a volley of slaps, administered in rapid succession and with great vigour. Any manifestation of emotion or of pain was an invitation to more blows. I managed, however, to obtain a vital concession. I explained to Koryasu, the elderly interpreter, that I wasn't so much objecting to the slaps, a normal practice in the Japanese forces, as saving my irreplaceable eyeglasses. I asked him, as a colleague, to petition the authorities that I be given warning before the blows fell. Koryasu came through. Prior to being hit, there would henceforth be a sharp order of "Glasses off!" Else, I was entitled to complain higher up, and on several occasions I did.

A reason for having my face slapped was failure to use the correct form of address. A major difficulty of Japanese is the complexity of honorifics. Depending on the rank and social circumstances of the speaker and his interlocutor, many words, verbs in particular, may change completely. Although the military, in their modes of address, tended towards simplification, proper grounding in the variants of the second person pronoun was critical. Some of the forms, however, found no place in my vocabulary. For example, *omae*, 'honorable in front', was superfluous: the pronoun is used when addressing people of a lower social status, and that included one's wife. In my case, neither existed.

I noticed that I was coming closer to understanding the substrate of the Japanese mind when a guard, having worked himself into a state of rage, spat at me the word *kisama*. I was appalled. I felt hurt and humiliated. I would far rather he had slapped me. Literally translated the word means "Honourable Lord in Front of Me". At one time it must have been the 'you' form that expressed the greatest respect. Now, used ironically, it has become one of the most insulting words in the language.

We tried to structure our leisure time. University courses were held daily, and we established special study groups. A thriving entertainment industry put on revues, musicals and plays, always well attended by the Japanese. I was on the lecture tour, my two set pieces being Proust and the London Stock Exchange. I was also a founder member of the Alpine Club, having on its behalf obtained permission from the Japanese to climb the highest and steepest rock-face in the Changi area. It had been hard to explain that the danger of snakes and the insufficiency of calories in our diet didn't, in this particular case, matter: to keep up our morale, sport was of uppermost importance. They thought us quite mad.

On a barter basis, I exchanged French conversation against lessons in celestial navigation with Lieutenant Colonel Julian Taylor, a celebrated London surgeon and yachtsman. Taylor had many interesting stories to tell, and none surpassed the circumstances connected with one of his early surgical interventions in camp.

He had been called in the middle of the night to save a man whose head had been partly severed by a sword blow. He was a soldier in his teens who had fallen into Japanese hands a few hours before surrender. Exceptionally, he was spared. The following day the officer commanding the unit that held him ordered a car and driver to take him to Changi. By evening, however, prisoner and driver were back, having failed to locate the P.O.W. camp. The officer, estimating that he had done more than enough, decapitated his prisoner.

It must have been a perfunctory blow, for some hours later the boy came to, covered with a loose and thin layer of earth. He managed to climb out of his grave. He was alone, the Japanese had gone. When he tried to move, he noticed that the muscles of his neck had been partly severed, making it necessary to steady his head between his hands. He stumbled into a nearby *kampong*.

From there, two Chinese villagers carried him to the edge of the Changi camp. He was discovered and rushed to the hospital. Only his extreme youth and his exceptional vitality enabled him to survive the shock and the loss of blood. A year later, he died of disease on the Siam-Burma railway.

Our numbers kept going down. No more than twelve or thirteen thousand men could have remained in Changi of the initial sixty thousand who had arrived in February '42, and of the twenty thousand Dutch who had come over from the Netherland East Indies. They had all gone 'up country', to Siam (or Thailand, no one knew exactly what the official appellation was) to work on the railway that ended up in Burma. Hardly any news filtered down from the north, yet we had a hunch that the status quo was highly desirable.

However when the Japanese announced that, because feeding us in Singapore was increasingly difficult, they planned to open up a model camp in the Cameron Highlands, the mountainous area in the centre of the Malay Peninsula, there was a scramble to be included in the party. We would be growing our own temperate-zone vegetables (the prospect of potatoes instead of rice was so heady that it could hardly be borne); meat was to be a daily item; malaria and beri-beri would be unknown; and, lastly, the camp would be open for inspection by the Red Cross. Although seven thousand men were to move to this paradise on earth, only two-thirds needed to be fit: there would be a 400-bed hospital for the sick. Anyway, it wouldn't have been possible to find seven thousand fit men in Changi.

We were told to take all the heavy luggage we wanted – stores, equipment, medicines, food, clothing, tools and kitchen utensils, even the steel *kwalis*, the three-foot wide woks, used to cook rice. To this were added two complete electric generators, as well as all the instruments for the "band", including a piano and a church harmonium.

F Force (3,334 British and 3,666 Australians) was to leave Singapore by mid-April under the command of Lieutenant Colonel Banno, a tall, grey-haired Japanese officer who had seen service in Sumatra and Manchuria. Banno was decent and ineffectual. Eventually the strain of bearing responsibility for the destruction of F Force made him almost senile.

Most of the remnants of the 18th Division were included in the British contingent. Three Japanese speakers went along. Cyril Wild, a major who had been a Shell executive in Japan, was the senior interpreter (he is the man carrying the white flag in the celebrated surrender photograph of General Percival and a group of staff officers on their way to meet the victor, General Yamashita, "The Tiger of Malaya"). The other interpreter had been an Eton schoolmaster. And I was of course picked by Colonel Hutchinson, to whom I was giving daily Japanese lessons. I had made no special effort to get on the bandwagon, but I was pleased to be going; it represented a a step closer, I thought, to implementing the three-and-a-half year dream and its promise of survival.

On April 18, 1943, the first of sixteen trains that were to carry F Force waited in a siding. The piano was loaded along with supplies of clothing, medicines and tinned food that we had saved since surrender for a rainy day. Thirty prisoners, and sometimes a Korean guard, were assigned to each of the ten-ton steel boxcars, seventeen feet long by seven wide, which, on an extended journey, could have accomodated nine men at a pinch. There wasn't even enough room to sit down. A sleeping, sitting and standing roster had to be established, but lying full length was never possible.

Three or four days later, my turn came to leave Singapore. After hours of waiting, the train got under way. The headquarters "rice-truck" (as we had dubbed the boxcars) was known as the "Pullman car". The Japanese sergeant in charge of the train and his half-dozen Koreans took up half the space; and the rest was occupied by Hutch, eight or nine British officers and myself.

Compared to the men in the other rice-trucks, we were travelling in luxury. But, like everyone else, we suffered from dehydration. The daily ration was a cup of water and a mess-tin of rice and soup. Once, (my diary is jubilant about the event), we detected shreds of meat in the liquid: we hadn't tasted anything like it in six months! During the day, the heat inside these steel boxes rose to 120 degrees. Even under way, although never at more than twenty miles per hour, the roof and sides were too hot to touch. We were drenched in sweat, and at night, we shivered with cold. Almost everyone had, if not dysentery, at least acute diarrhoea.

When the train was under way, for *benjo* (Japanese for lavatory, one of the two words everyone knew along with *yasume*, rest), it was necessary to project one's rear end out of the door, while clinging on to a chain stretched across the opening. Someone had to keep a lookout for bridges or tunnels and, literally, save your arse.

At stops, in stations or in the open country, we tumbled out of the train to squat and groan along the tracks. Sometimes I managed to talk the guards and the engineer into letting us draw water from the steam locomotive. It was oily and smelly. But it was wet. (Another madeleine, auditory this time: the sound of steam and boiling water coming out from a tap and the promise of relief from thirst.)

The possibility that we had been hoodwinked slowly arose in our minds. The certainty was revealed at Ipoh, where we should have detrained for the Cameron Highlands. Instead, the doors of headquarters truck opened, the Japanese got out, shouts and screams filled the air and thirty Indian coolies were pushed into our space. In an instant our Pullman car had become the most loathsome place in the whole train. Pandemonium followed as we attempted to reorganise ourselves. I was jammed in a corner, trampled by bare feet, overcome by a noxious stench, a compound of disease, ordure and sweat. From under, I plaintively bleated out a ridiculous sound: "How can these bloody Nips allow this to happen?" Hutch's voice was heard, like a whip cracking across the packed bodies: "For Christ's sake, Ullmann, stop moaning like a bloody old woman!" I stopped.

The cat was out of the bag: Adieu piano! Adieu potatoes! We were on our way to the Siam-Burma railway. Hope flew out of the truck doors along with notes of Malay currency issued by the Japanese: certain that they would be unacceptable wherever we were going, the men scattered them like dead leaves in the wind. Louis stopped such foolishness: astutely thinking that the Japanese occupation scrip would be interchangeable throughout the occupied territories, he collected the supposedly useless currency, promising to pay back its owners at the rate of 50 Malay dollars for one Thai tical. He kept his promise and his journey turned out to be highly profitable.

We continued our way north through the Kra Isthmus and crossed into Thailand. On the fifth day, we were shunted to a siding. The heat rose. The Indians were half comatose. Some were near death. Urine and faeces sloshed on the hot steel floor. We had received nothing to eat or drink for twenty-four hours. It was my turn to push my nose out of the doors, cracked open a couple of inches (the rule when we stopped close to a station) and I was trying to get a draught of cool air, when another train pulled in next to ours. It was laden with Thai troops. At that moment I received the greatest present of my life, almost the gift of life itself. An arm came out through the doors of the rice-truck alongside. The face belonging to the arm was invisible, but the hand held out a slice of water-melon. In a marvellous symmetry, I stretched out my own arm and grasped the cool, moist fruit, glowing supernaturally in the penumbra of the two wagons.

II

THERE

FIVE

(1943)

When it reaches the little town called Banpong the railway line that has been running due north for a thousand miles makes a sharp ninety-degree turn towards Bangkok, forty miles to the East. Banpong was our destination.

The country was dead flat, with the geometrical pattern of paddy fields broken up by clumps of pawpaws, plantains and tapioca. Kapok trees spread out their long limbs at right angles to the bare trunks, like surrealistic candelabras; while elegant areca and nipa palms swayed against the blue sky reflected in the still waters of the paddy fields. From our boxcars, we waved at the tiny children leading herds of black water-buffalo.

The train slowed down and stopped at a siding. We fell out of the rice-trucks, stiff, hungry, clotted with sweat and filth. We extracted the sick and unloaded our gear. Everyone picked up as much as he could carry and staggered along the mile of road to the staging camp.

The arrival of F Force had turned Banpong into a boom town. For a few unscrupulous Thais there was the prospect of fleecing us of everything we owned. For everyone else there were stores to be looted as soon as we were on our way, and in the meantime the opportunity to buy most of our gear – too heavy to lug on the march – at absurd prices. Miraculously, these heaven-sent opportunities were daily renewed. It was a happy crowd that followed the ragged column of men, bent under the weight of equipment, through the dingy little town.

If you looked up from below your load, however, the immediate prospects were mouthwatering. Varied and succulent foods were displayed in extravagant abundance. Shopkeepers and stall-owners were handing out sticky cakes, bananas (pink and tiny, or deep-fried in a sweet batter), sticks of roasted meat and pieces of coconut. The tricycle rickshaw boys offered free rides; and the mamas were running along the column displaying the young girls awaiting our pleasure. It certainly wasn't the cool Cameron Highlands and the dream camps (the pre-monsoon heat was stifling), but it wasn't drab. And drabness is the bane of the P.O.W.'s existence. "First impressions of Siam excellent," says my diary.

Second impressions were decidedly less so. What was visible of the camp from afar was a vast area enveloped in swirling dust. Through the dust, like Chinese shadows, hundreds of prisoners were being herded about like disorientated sheep. The Japanese were waving bamboo sticks, bellowing orders and barking curses.

We passed through the gate. The notice above its transom described without ambiguity the place we were entering: Transit Camp for Cattle, Coolies and Prisoners-of-War. Dead trees stood about. Vultures sat on their bare limbs.

A dreadful foulness had seeped into that minute speck of the world. Underfoot, filth and latrine trenches overflowing with maggots and excrement; in the air, fat green flies and mosquitoes; and in the bamboo huts, lice and bedbugs. The man who *de facto* ruled this foulness was Toyama, a Korean auxiliary, a *heiko*. Toyama was immaculate, lithe, hyperactive and dangerous. He exuded a strong sexual aura. His skin, matte and pale, was as smooth as a woman's. The eyes, slitted and deep black, darted incessantly over the prisoner he was about to hit, as if searching for a weak spot. His voice at odd moments reached almost a coloratura pitch, and at others came down to a passionate hiss. He was complex and uncontrollable; his lover, Lieutenant Fukuda, who was actually in charge of the Banpong camp, had no power over him. Toyama's homosexuality appeared fused to sadism – with sadism in the role of the paramount pleasure principle. At all times, in his right hand, he held a golf club. He went about looking for people to hit: he needed to hurt as others need companionship. Like a cobra, he struck at me the moment I had passed the gate and he learned that I spoke Japanese. He whacked me on the side of the head. Light exploded in front of my eyes, stars shot into my brain, and I was filled with a rage that I barely controlled. I nicknamed him "Niblick", and the name stuck right to the end of the war.

From the two previous train parties still in camp, we learned that the hated Kempeitai were about to pounce and carry out a thorough search. Then they broke the news: the work areas marked out for F Force were on the Burma border. Without transport and with almost half of the men sick, we would have to cover 200 miles of jungle tracks on foot.

The only water point for the whole camp, a well by the cookhouse, was already half-filled with revolvers, ammunition, compasses, daggers and all manners of prohibited articles that the prisoners had jettisoned. We added our contribution, but Captain Mudie who had installed the Changi receiving set, managed to save the small radio he had brought along. He had disguised it as a flashlight. Its large battery case contained a miniaturised radio, the bulb itself being lit by a small penlight cell. As torches were liable to be confiscated, Mudie threw away the bulb and reflector part, hiding the vital component in his clothes. Understandably, after our train journey, the Kempeitai didn't relish bodily contact with us, and only kits were searched.

The trading between Thais and P.O.W.s was extensive and incessant. Even at those moments when it was necessary to negotiate the slimy bamboos over the maggot-filled *benjo*, native buyers would suddenly materialise out of the bushes, squat by your side and start negotiations. The bushes were also animated with séances of "jig-a-jig". The accepted rate was five minutes with a young girl for a pair of long trousers, whereas shorts would provide a thirty-year-old; and the mamas themselves would be happy with a pair of socks. Sex had promptly reappeared along with a well filled stomach.

Most of my time was taken up in disputes involving guards, prisoners and local traders. The Japanese consigned the goods they had confiscated to the guard-room, but inexplicably, the following day, they dumped them back on me for return to their original owners. A posse of muscular Thais would be waiting in ambush. They wrenched my burden away from me, and bid furiously for its contents. I escaped, scattering part of the goods behind me. As most often the owner had departed, I simply added his belongings to a large pile of gear that was being daily and systematically looted.

My own kit was twice stolen, but replacing it was, of course, no problem: everything was there for the picking. From one of the medical officers I received a piece of advice that probably later saved my life. It was to take from the stores a couple of jars of Marmite, a vegetable spread extremely rich in vitamins of the B-complex category; never to discard them; and to open them only when I came down with beri-beri. I'd never liked the stuff, and I still don't. But it did what the doctor promised.

Lieutenant Colonel Harris, commander of F Force, and his headquarter officers left Banpong by truck. Rear-headquarters (to which I became interpreter once Cyril Wild had gone off with Harris) remained behind to supervise the trainloads still to arrive from Singapore. Our most valuable stores were taken off to be stored in a building by the station, and we received assurances from Colonel Banno that the invalid food, clothing and medicines would be promptly sent up to Nikki, the base camp of F Force.

Two weeks later, rear H.Q.'s job was over, and we left – Lieutenant Colonel Houston, our chief medical officer, three majors and myself – perched on top of a truck. The date was May 7, and the time 10 a.m.

I was perfectly conscious of the incredible privilege of not being on foot like everyone else, carrying a heavy pack. Looking down from my eminence at the men below, I experienced the proverbial superiority of the cavalry over the infantry.

Yet another part of me said "You're a traitor to your class." I was, after all, an "other rank" – a creature who didn't hold the King's Commission – and sitting precariously on a pile of luggage I appeared to be on an equal footing, so to speak, with a colonel and three majors. The gap beween a wartime corporal/acting sergeant (Intelligence Corps, moreover, not precisely a posh regiment) and a regular army colonel was as great as that between a bus driver and the pilot of a Formula I Ferrari. I had to remind myself that there'd been a slight malfunction in the machinery of fate; if all had gone according to Major Gielgud's plan, I would have picked up my commission in Cairo, and by now I would, in all probability, be a full lieutenant. Lest that argument be thought too hypothetical, said another part of myself, then all these ignorant other-ranks who couldn't even number off correctly in Nippon-go should remind themselves that I often got hit on their behalf, and that surely evened out the score.

The truck was loaded with large wicker trunks. They contained the only medical supplies that would ever reach the camps on the Burma border.

No sooner had we turned off on the road leading to Kanchanaburi than a splendid looting party got under way in Banpong. The P.O.W.s left behind to guard the stores joined forces with the Japanese. The Thais bought up all the goods they could get. Everyone prospered.

The piano, I heard much later, ended up in the café next to the station.

(1979)
Maybe it's only a premonition, but this time I think I'll succeed. My plan is to go all the way to the Kwai and its catchment area, to the Three Pagodas Pass.

Once before I'd made a stab at it. It was in April 1978, ten months ago. As April is the hottest month of the year, rather than spend two hours in this train rattling and swaying from Bangkok to Kanchanaburi, I had boarded the Class A luxury bus in Bangkok.

It wasn't only the heat but also the memory of the "rice-trucks" of P.O.W. days; I couldn't resist the enticements of comfort. The air-conditioning in the Mercedes-Benz bus was individually controlled; the seats were adjustable to a half prone position; the hostesses wore pert uniforms, and flashing the proverbial Thai smile, they offered complimentary drinks. Lastly, I had the perverse pleasure of observing above the driver (black tie, white shirt and white gloves) a modern, mobile sacrarium – a small Sony colour television set flanked by a portrait of their majesties, the King and Queen of Thailand, and of the Lord Buddha. Garlands of fresh and plastic flowers festooned and unified the shrine's disparate elements.

Riding the bus, however, had been a mistake. If I wanted to summon up the remembrance of things past, I had to select a mode of travel in harmony with my purpose. Invoking the spirits has always required a specific ritual, and I had disregarded the rule. Nor had the omens been encouraging. "No, you can't go," I'd been told in Bangkok by the vestals and the oracles at the Thai Organisation for Tourism, known as T.O.T. "We'd like to help you. We understand why you want to go up there. But we don't want to lose you. No one goes into the River Kwai area. Except Communist guerillas and bandits. It's a bad place: lots of disease and wild beasts." I didn't believe a word of it. I insisted so much, however, that they agreed to give me a guide. "But," said the chief vestal, a relative of the Queen of Thailand, "I think you're on a sticky wicket." She'd spent a long time working in the London T.O.T. bureau.

A young Thai from T.O.T. whose name had a distant phonetic affinity with "Peter" (which he requested immediately he be addressed by) met me at the Kanchanaburi bus station. He had reserved two seats on a VW Microbus due to depart that afternoon. We left three days later. Astonishingly, we went as far north as Tha-Khanun, 100 miles from Kanchanaburi, and halfway to the Burma border. The drive had taken an excruciating thirteen hours. The wheels ploughed a deep ribbon of dust which had both the consistency and the aspect of finely ground flour. The windows were kept firmly closed and caulked with old rags. In spite of all our precautions white eddies whirled around the passengers, who soon looked like Venetian Pierrots.

We moved through a white-out; the rays of the sun were diffused by the dust cloud thrown up by our wheels, and as the vegetation on both sides of the track was thickly coated with the inert and cloying stuff, we slowly groped our way along a white tunnel. Not only did we suffocate in the heat, not only were we gagged by the dust and bounced along ruts when we weren't trying to pull the car out of them, but we also had to endure the driver's personal collection of rock-and-pop tapes booming at a high level of decibels. As a prisoner, I had known worse moments on the road to the Three Pagodas, but not many.

The morning after our arrival at Tha-Khanun, Peter came to say that the District Officer wanted to see me. I had noticed looming above the village trees a radio mast, and I'd had a fleeting thought that the airwaves might have brought a message from Bangkok concerning my plans. I was proved right. The D.O. was all smiles. Tea was served, little cakes were offered, and he asked if he could help me in any way.

Unfortunately, to his recollection, no one had tried reaching the Three Pagodas Pass in years. For one thing there was only a few miles of road north of Tha-Khanun, and beyond nothing but a hazardous track. If a jeep driver agreed to attempt the journey, he could charge no less, he warned us, than the equivalent of 2,000 U.S. Dollars: the vehicle would have to be taken apart at the end of the trip and completely overhauled. We would find it far more agreeable, added the D.O., to go and visit a nearby lake. I declined, and two days later Peter and I were back in Kanchanaburi.

This time T.O.T. haven't been told anything. Jacques Bes, a Frenchman who runs a raft hotel on the Kwai, seventy-five miles up from Kanchanaburi, has promised to help. The plan is first to reach Kanchanaburi by train; and then ride the narrow-gauge line (the "Death Railway" or what's left of it) to its terminus at Nam Tok. Bes's Thai-Chinese wife who takes care of the office in Bangkok has confirmed that her husband will be there, waiting for me. By boat we'll go up the Kwai to the rafts at Kinsaiyok, the 172 Kilo mark (on the kilometre scale that we all used at the time, starting at Banpong, the head of the line). From Kinsaiyok on, Bes will take me in hand and try to get me to the Three Pagodas.

Peter, last year's T.O.T. guide (unofficially told of my arrival), meets me at the Kanchanaburi train station.

(P.O.W. Diary)
In Kanburi [Kanchanaburi] we stopped for an hour in the crowded streets, waiting for the arrival of Col. Banno whose lorry we were to follow. Kanburi is an old town surrounded by a red stone wall, and it doesn't have the shabby and tawdry appearance of Banpong, a boom place grown suddenly into a base for the projected railway.

We sat on top of our Marmon [a type of lorry captured from the British] watching the East go by – the rich Thais in their American cars and the leprous beggars crouching in corners; the prosperous Chinese *towkay* rocking in a chair by the entrance of his shop, and the lean coolie jog-trotting with his heavy burden slung on a bamboo pole. Dashing in and out of the crowd, busy on some urgent errand, numerous Buddhist monks, in bright orange robes, their shaven heads gleaming in the sunlight. We said little but we all thought that this was likely to be the last time we would see anything larger than a jungle village for a very long time.

More than three decades separate the diary's Somerset Maugham scene and what I observe on the way to Peter's house. In conformity with many provincial towns of the Third World, it would appear that the care and nurturing of pick-up trucks is at the core of human activity. The goods they move, the people who drive them and those who repair and service them are, you might believe, merely ancillary to the existence of the machines themselves.

Like horses tethered at the rail outside the sheriff's office in a Western movie, the pick-ups are arrayed off the street flank to flank, their bonnets nuzzling the cinder blocks of mean, one-storey buildings in the international shoe-box style of architecture.

Three wheeled *samlans*, the Vespa-type taxis that have replaced the tricycle rickshaws, race ten-wheeler Mercedes-Benz trucks down the main street. The noise has the quality of pulsating ectoplasm; the air vibrates and generates more heat. Apart from the gleam of a golden stupa glimpsed through a thicket of TV aerials and ascending clouds of diesel fumes, and the ever-present appearance of elephants on posters advertising toothpaste or agricultural machinery, the noise is the surest indication that this is Thailand, where the tampering with or outright removal of mufflers is the first action taken after purchasing a device equipped with an internal combustion engine. This love of mechanical racket, I'm convinced, is the antidote to the silent diffidence in which the Thais wrap themselves when speaking to one another.

Another object of care and nurturing in Kanchanaburi is the myth of *The Bridge on the River Kwai*. The steel bridge itself (across the River Kwae Yai, the Little Kwai, for there's not a single bridge spanning the Big, or real, Kwai known as the River Kwae Noi), although quite unlike the wooden one destroyed in the movie has become a tourist attraction where the Bangkok train makes a special stop.

The C56 Class wood-fired pony engine ("built by the Oigawa Railway Company"), and a diesel truck equipped with flanged wheels so that it can run on rails, stand as a monument on their own length of track. A bronze plaque tells the bare facts:

started October 1942, completed October 1943, 450 kilometres long.

Close by a stone stela has been erected, dedicated to the men of all nationalities who perished building the railway.

Away from the river a large cemetery is impeccably laid out and maintained. Flamboyants and hibiscus spread over the gravestones. I read the names of the farm boys who enlisted in the 18th Division's East Anglian units – the Bedfords, the Cambridgeshires, the Norfolk Yeomanry and the Suffolk Regiment. The names are mostly a pious sham. Perhaps in the base camps men were buried singly and records were kept, but up country, where most died and where from the huge funeral pyres a few random fragments of bones and a pinch of ashes were gathered, identification was impossible. "A man who died for his country" is the complete inscription on several graves. It sounds truer.

It's Sunday and Thai families, with their children and picnic baskets, have come to spend the day in the cemetery, the cleanest and neatest park, perhaps the only park, of Kanchanaburi.

Japanese tourists walk slowly and in silence, until the moment of photography when their composure gives way to babble, gesturing and argumentation. As soon as everyone has been cajoled and manoeuvred into a precise and immutable position, the Thai guide starts clicking shutters: at his feet lie as many cameras as there are Japanese in front of him. He picks up one camera after the other, exposes one frame, and places it aside. Everyone will have his very own record of the cemetery.

Dressed in black, a group of large Dutchmen also take photographs. Their next stop is the war cemetery of Thambuyzayat in Burma, the other end of the line. It's the president of the Dutch War Grave Commission's third visit here. "Yes," he says, "the young in Holland are intrigued by the war. This gives them an idea."

Further down and accessible by boat is a smaller cemetery, Chung Kai. The sun is low. The flowers, mauve, pink and white, catch the last rays and glow against the long shadows on the ground. Facing the setting sun, a rooster crows.

The following day I visit the Chichumpol P.O.W. Museum, set up and cared for by a local Buddhist monastery. Large drawings depict the more spectacularly unpleasant aspects of our lives. Disturbed, I observe the crude renditions of tortures, forced marches, cholera, latrines, even a visit to the dentist (no anaesthetics). A vitrine displays "archaeological" remains, a radio, a railway spike, a knife, a bomb fragment. A young monk (Pradirek Mahapunyo – I get a Christmas card every year) comes and explains. I cut him short. "I was there," I say, pointing out the camp marked Sonkurai on the three-dimensional model of the railway that has been laid outdoors under a notice, Notorious Camps.

In the restaurant by the bridge, I sit at a table in front of an iced beer. Booklets, T-shirts, postcards and slides celebrate a site consecrated by a film that a good proportion of the planet's population has seen. "The tourists will definitely have the joy of their life cruising along the real River Kwai on the way to pay a visit to the Chungkai War Memorial Cemetery." I'm tired and I feel empty. From my French schooldays I remember Bergson noting the difference between mere recollection of facts and their emotional reliving. What come to mind now are episodes, anecdotes, times of elation and times of despair. But all connection between memory and emotion has been severed. I feel nothing.

In the little train to Nam Tok, I revive. This stretch of line, 75 miles long out of a total of 250 built by the prisoners, is all that's left of the Siam-Burma Railway. We start very slowly over the steel bridge with its original arched spans. Square ones in the centre replace those destroyed in the British and American air attacks of 1944–45.

There's not a tourist aboard the train, only peasants returning to their holdings. Women move through the carriages selling from their baskets irresistible foods wrapped in leaves, skewered on slivers of wood, or stuffed inside bamboo sticks. A smiling boy is offering acid-green and shocking-pink sweet drinks in soft plastic pouches.

The railway line follows the river's left bank. The Kwai is brown and sluggish. A houseboat, atap roofed, is anchored midstream: a cow stands in the stern, chickens pecking between her feet. Water buffalo wallow in the mud. A punt drifts with the current, and kingfishers skim the surface of the water. The cultivated land is reduced to a thin, intermittent strip along the railway line. Beyond the river, the dark and billowy jungle spreads out to the hills. I'm reminded of the Indian saying, "Wisdom settles along the banks of a large river."

THERE

I look up the diary for this part of the journey:

Col. Banno's Marmon arrived [in Kanchanaburi], took the lead and we followed it. The metalled road soon petered out into a jungle track, villages gave way to small, isolated farms nestling under tall betel-nut palms. We passed several working camps of P.O.W.s. The river was crossed on a wide wooden bridge. Hundreds of prisoners were working on another steel bridge that looked almost completed.

The road wound in and out of thick jungle. It was nothing more than three or four parallel ruts cut by numerous streams. We began to realise the hardships of the night marches. Already, in Kanburi, over a hundred men of F Force had been abandoned. They were in the open, sleeping under bushes, and without drugs.

Towards 6 p.m. we arrived at a huge encampment in the jungle, surrounded by a picket fence – hundreds of huts, tents, and workshops, a main supply base for the new railway.

It was called Ta Sao. We spent the night here, under canvas with our Jap drivers, and shared their food and their liquor.

The engine's whistle echoes between the walls of the ninety-foot deep cuttings at Arrow Hill (108 Kilo). For five months, five hundred men dug vertically into the rock, working night and day. Few survived.

At 114 Kilo, the train slows down to a crawl and crosses the Wampo viaducts. For a thousand feet they cling to the cliff forming an S-bend. A criss-cross of teak posts supports the shelf. Everyone hangs out of the windows. I jump out of the train and walk. Here, like at Arrow Hill, for every sleeper laid down a dozen men died. The river, way below, curves west. Dense jungle hugs the banks. At last, this is the Kwai I remember.

At Nam Tok (Tha Soe camp and P.O.W. hospital), the end of the line, Jacques Bes is waiting for me by the track.

SIX

(1943)
Tha Soe (or Nam Tok) was, when we saw it, the line's farthest and most important base.

Our arrival coincided with the start of the "speedo" phase. *"Kora! Speedo!"* became the incantation heard up and down the line. "Speedo" justified driving prisoners and coolies to their deaths in order to accelerate the construction of the railway. Originally eighteen months had been scheduled for its completion, but early in '43 Tokyo decreed that it was to become operational by October, six months earlier. The "speedo" orders, we were told, emanated from the Emperor himself. *"Any sick man who staggers to the line to lay a sleeper will not have died in vain,"* encapsulated nicely the Engineers' philosophy.

The railway was needed to mount the Japanese offensive against India. The High Command in Tokyo knew that in time the Allied navies would regain control of the Bay of Bengal. Rangoon, Burma's capital and port of entry for the troops and supplies destined for the invasion of India, would then be blockaded. However, once the Thai and Burmese railway systems had become linked, war material could be unloaded in Bangkok and shipped overland to the front – India's Assam border.

Surveyors were secretly dispatched to the Kwai basin to draw up a feasibility report even before the Imperial Japanese Armies had completed their invasions of Thailand and Burma. It wasn't the first time that the idea had come up; before the war the British had considered an identical project. But the difficulties had been found too great: the jungle, after the Amazon, is the densest in the world; the terrain is hilly and criss-crossed by streams; malaria and cholera are endemic. But for the I.J.A., unlike the British, the human cost didn't count much; they could call on a vast body of prisoners, as well as over 100,000 native levies recruited in Thailand, Burma, India and Indochina.

At Tha Soe, much to our surprise, our little group, rear H.Q., joined up with H.Q. proper. Colonel Harris and his entourage had been ordered to stay put. Why, no one ever discovered. It wrecked, in effect, the little that could have been done effectively to try and comfort our men on their way to the camps up north.

So far, travelling by truck, we had seen little of the hardships of the journey on foot, and never experienced them personally. But at Tha Soe, for the first time, we saw columns of unfit and undernourished men wrecked by the forced marches.

Evening fell, and the men of No. 7 Train arrived, depleted in numbers, strung out and exhausted. Colonel Banno stood by, watching them. A prisoner staggered and fell unconscious at his feet. Banno, visibly upset, called for Colonel Houston, our chief medical officer. He had, he said with emotion in his voice, the greatest concern for the health of the prisoners under his care. Well, he was told, his concern was appreciated, but how could we alleviate their suffering? It was up to the Japanese to supply food and medicine, and to cut down the forced marches.

We were back to the basics of the situation. The trek would have been hard slogging for fit men; in our case, at least a third of the prisoners were sick, had been sick when they left Singapore, and everyone suffered from malnutrition, malaria and dysentery. There wasn't much that Houston or any other doctor could do.

When Houston's group (of which I was still part) was ordered on its way, the H.Q. officers were outraged: what, allow *rear* H.Q. to take the lead? Major Wild appealed to Banno, who relented. Not much, however; only Colonel Harris would be allowed to go ahead, and he was to ride on our truck. The palaver continued, producing endless orders and counter-orders. Whatever the merits of the case, for the wartime soldiers watching the professionals of both camps slogging it out, motivated by what we saw as military pique, the situation was at the same time comical and infuriating.

We bumped along a rutted track, past gangs of British, Australian and Dutch prisoners working alongside native coolies. After fifteen miles, the leading truck, with Banno riding in the cab, stopped in a clearing. Banno signalled for me to come over.

Colonel Harris, he said, would join him and together they would ride to Nikki, the base camp for F Force. As for us, rear H.Q., we were to unload the medical supplies here in Kanyu (162 Kilo) and tend to the columns that would be passing through on their way north. As the trunks contained mostly surgical supplies the plan was nonsensical. Once again, we tried to have the order rescinded. I called on all the persuasiveness I was capable of, but the decision stuck. No doubt the I.J.A. military manual specified something about First Aid Posts, and it had to be implemented. The guards screamed at us to unload the stores. They kept up their imprecations until the job was completed. It was their way, we supposed, to show off their martial ardour in front of their commanding officer.

The last we saw of poor Colonel Harris, commander of F Force, was his forlorn-looking silhouette perched atop Banno's truck, clutching a suitcase filled with tins of food and medicines. The truck lurched off into the darkness of the jungle and was soon out of sight.

The choice of the clearing in which we'd been dumped had been determined by the presence of a small stream. Bamboos two feet in diameter soared to a feathery canopy where the sunlight flickered yellow and gold. But at ground level we lived in a perpetual semi-twilight. In the slightest breeze, the bamboo creaked and groaned like the spars of a sailing ship. In a half gale, the din was terrifying; the hollow trunks boomed and clanked until you thought the forest was about to collapse on you.

A few hundred yards away, a detachment of a dozen Japanese commanded by an elderly corporal lived in a tent mounted on a platform. The corporal had a long, sad face, and we nicknamed him Disraeli.

Disraeli ordered us to put up a hospital (a tarpaulin in shreds spread taut to form a roof), and to build a cookhouse. From a nearby camp a few British and Australians came to help.

The columns struggled in as dawn broke. The men had been marching for twelve or fourteen hours but on arrival they were immediately put to digging latrines and refuse pits, taking care of the sick and cooking. Occasionally, they had been attacked by Thai bandits. At roll-call, one or more men might be found missing, killed for a watch or a piece of worn army clothing. The Koreans were so frightened that they handed their rifles over to the prisoners and stayed well inside the column. After their meal of rice, onion-water and tiny shreds of buffalo meat, the prisoners laid themselves down on the ground and went to sleep. In the evening they were counted again, a few beatings were haphazardly distributed, and they were sent on their way, leaving behind only the desperately ill.

Disraeli and his men gave us no trouble. More, they went out of their way to please us. They took us to hot springs, five miles away, down precipitous ravines, by the banks of the Kwai. The Japanese demonstrated how they immersed themselves very slowly in the scalding water. We tried it, and they roared with happiness when they heard our screams of pain. On the way back, we stopped at the canteen of a P.O.W. camp. We heard stories of overcrowding, ruthless guards, and a greedy Chinese contractor. A small cemetery was fast filling up.

The last of the F Force columns came and went. Our privileged existence ended. Now it was our turn to leave the clearing. But there was no transport, neither for us nor for the medical supplies which would have to be abandoned. Colonel Houston and Major Agnew, who both had suppurating feet, stayed behind with a dozen sick men.

We left on May 23, the two other majors and myself. We were glad to be off: after thousands of men had gone through the clearing where sanitation was non-existent, fat, black flies swarmed around us in ever-thicker clouds. Life in Kanyu became unbearable, and we all contracted dysentery.

It was our first experience of the march, and by the time we reached Kinsayok, only twelve miles away, we had jettisoned a good part of our belongings. Our worldly goods were going to be whittled down even more in the near future.

(1979)

Jacques looks the part to perfection as he climbs into a battered Land Rover loaded with supplies for the rafts: grey curly hair, a scar on his chin; a towel knotted around his neck, green bush shirt, khaki shorts and flip-flops on his feet. Before starting on the journey to Kinsaiyok and the rafts we go and have a Singha beer with a plate of chicken wings at a restaurant overlooking the river.

We load up the two long-tailed boats and we roar off upstream. From the six-cylinder Chrysler engine amidships, a ten-foot propeller shaft extends to the rear, its angle allowing the slim boat to navigate shallows. When the sun hits the spume arcing off the stern, the boat trails a splendid rainbow. Except for the tremendous noise (music to Thai ears), the craft in those moments resembles an oversized and wildly iridescent dragonfly.

The journey to Kinsaiyok takes almost two hours, winding through a corridor of thick vegetation. All along the banks a dull grey-green creeper grows out of the water, reminiscent of mangrove. "Not mangrove," shouts Jacques over the Chrysler, "it's *Khrai Nam – Homonoia Riparia* to you." Above the bamboo thickets, the Yang or Ironwood Tree spreads its dark green fronds.

The first of many white calcarous cones, the geologist's inselberg, rises around a bend, and the river looks like a Chinese print. A buffalo scampers up the banks. A grey punt, from which a man and a woman are fishing, rocks in our wake. Waterfalls crash into the river and swifts streak out of limestone caves.

Past and present now connect. Images coalesce, those of 1943 and of 1979.

Looking down (when I was a prisoner) on that river at dawn, fog skimming the water, mist ascending in soft billows over the jungle; listening to the cries of invisible birds, and sometimes hearing the distant trumpeting of an elephant, helped one to remember the first commandment, *Primum Vivere*. The experience, just like the sun that was soon to dispel fog and mist, cleared doubts at those moments when hopelessness pushed you down the dark and slippery tunnel. The reaffirmation came seldom. But when it did, it brought a great silence. At the time, I equated this silence with happiness, and I could have been absolutely right.

One more bend in the river, and the rafts come into view. Six of them, looking like houseboats, with an atap hut perched on each raft. An old steam launch with a tall black-and-white funnel is moored alongside. An elephant is drinking his fill at the water's edge.

Cans of iced beer are handed out in the centre raft which serves as dining-room and bar. From my deckchair I look right across the river. "Look over there, on the other bank," Jacques says, "that's where the Kinsaiyok camp used to be."

THERE

(1943)

Kinsaiyok was a huge sprawling camp by the river. It housed several thousand P.O.W.s from previous parties, as well as some fifty British and Australians from F Force who had dropped out of their groups, and were now fit enough to resume the march. Many huts were empty, and yet, as had been the case since Kanchanaburi, we were not allowed to enter them. Was it, we wondered, a Japanese rule or simply bloody-mindedness?

We went down the river for a wash, and for the first time we heard the terrible word – *cholera*. So far it was only a rumour. Further up the line, it was said, men had been struck down. Not for long, however, for almost everyone died within forty-eight hours.

On our way up we had skirted one or two deserted villages. Notices in Thai and Japanese were pasted on walls. We guessed their content: one word was in English, Cholera. The disease was endemic to the country. Those responsible for its spread to F Force, said the British, were the devil-may-care, irresponsible Aussies who drank the river water even though they'd been warned against it. The Aussies blamed the Poms who were filthy, who never washed. For lack of greater precision the subject was dropped. The immediate challenge, in any case, was the monsoon. Heavy, gibbous clouds were daily rolling in, and the dark sky was filled with threat. The heat became oppressive.

The marching parties always slept in the open. By the time the rains came, the working camps south of the Three Pagoda Pass would have been reached. And there, surely, shelter was ready. But this was not to be.

Early afternoon of May 25, I found Major R., with whom I'd formed a friendship (he was among the sick left behind at Kinsaiyok), looking at the clouds and sniffing the wind. R. had worked in the teak forests of Burma. He knew the climate. "It's for tonight," he said. "We'd better get going." Bamboo was always plentiful, but in the coming days our well-being would always depend on finding wild banana leaves; it wasn't otherwise possible to make a waterproof roof. To lash down the bamboo poles, as we possessed no string, we used bits of rags or lianas that we tore off the trees with bare hands. The lean-to was carefully positioned so that the opening faced away from the wind.

The monsoon season opened shortly after midnight with a thunderstorm of operatic extravagance. Bolts of lightning illuminated the jungle like magnesium flares. As the thunder exploded, the air itself felt as if it had shattered into its different elements, ionised and unstable. The metallic reek of ozone obliterated all the jungle odours. The wind howled in the jungle canopy, and in the bamboo thickets the hollow boles boomed and clanged.

Shafts of rain lashed our fragile shelter. We hung on to it like two men clinging to a raft, shouting to make ourselves heard. The shafts turned into sheets of water and the lean-to collapsed on top of us. We curled up in the foetal position, and remained under the débris. When our kit started floating away (we had failed to take terrain into consideration, and we were in a hollow), we struggled out. We waited for the dawn, huddled and shivering at the foot of a tree.

For ten days the rain fell. With every short respite, fat clouds of steam wreathed the undergrowth and crept up to the canopy. The air itself became acqueous, and in the vaporous silence we slowly came back to life. Within forty-eight hours the river flooded the adjacent jungle. Six months later the monsoon season finally ended.

(1979)

After dinner, a map is laid out on the dining room table. Jacques confirms the rumour I've heard in Bangkok: there's another bridge still standing on the Burmese side of the border. Whether I'll be able to reach it depends on the military situation. Mon guerillas and regular army patrols engage in occasional firefights along the border areas. Government troops can suddenly decide to carry out a sweep, and it's only when I reach the Three Pagodas Pass, Phra Chedi as it's known from here on, that the guerillas will decide whether it's safe to go in.

The Mons are one of the seven main ethnic groups which have been opposing the central government in Rangoon since 1948. They are fighting, they say, for a separatist state and complete independence. The least they will accept is equal status in the Federation of Burma but they don't believe in the promises of the majority. Many have fled their country for Thailand. About fifteen refugee families live in a settlement that Jacques has built on the hill at the back of the rafts. He's known as a friend of the Mons, and this will be a great help along my journey. A young Mon, Aung Song, will be my guide.

When darkness falls, a dozen villagers come down to the rafts and sing. Two young girls dance. Their fragile, elongated hands catch the flicker of flames, and move with the grace of aquatic grasses weaving in a stream. In the trees, out of the circle of light, gibbons chatter and play, waiting for everyone to go to bed so that they can raid the kitchen for leftovers.

I wake up in the middle of the night, walk out of my hut and pee into the river. The waxing moon is reflected in the water. I listen to the night sounds, but apart from the intermittent three notes of a bird I can't identify, all I hear is the munching and shuffling of the two old elephants who are spending their retirement years in the Bes compound. The male is nervous and not yet able to apply himself to any task. One night, a year ago, four men arrived by boat, went ashore and stunned him with car batteries. They sawed off his tusks and made their getaway. The Mons (and Jacques) have sworn to find them and kill them.

Breakfast over, Aung Song takes me across the river. He wants to show me an old campsite. After a twenty-minute walk we reach a clearing. Aung Song points out piled-up sacks of cement, rock-hard and fungus-covered; and cement blocks embedded in the ground, the remains of a well and its pump. He mentions another relic that I won't bother to go and see: five miles downstream, he says, one of the steel "rice-trucks" stands at the edge of the jungle. It's now the village jail.

A dozen sleepers, surprisingly intact, are still lined up on the ground – part of the railway bed to Tha-Khanun. When the war was over, the Thais came up by boat with acetylene torches, and cut up the track. Elephants hauled the rails to the river, and they were loaded on to barges. The railway ended up as scrap.

Three years ago Jacques built his raft hotel and his own abode, a tree house, up the hill, next to the Mon village. The Mon refugees who don't cultivate the land work for him. The cooks have been taught to prepare French dishes. Not to try and duplicate them, but to adapt them to the local produce. Culinary strains of Burmese origin make an unexpected appearance in an *estouffade de buffle*; and a Kwai *bouillabaisse* (carp, murrell and catfish) is flavoured with lemon grass instead of saffron. A distinct French cultural presence has installed itself on this bend of the river. So much so that one of the mahouts has been taught to speak a little French. (Did he start off, I wonder, with *"Nos ancêtres les Gaulois"?*) Two women from the French Embassy in Bangkok occupy the raft next to mine. At table, one of them reminisces about life in Cambodia, when at the end of the day's work the embassy staff in Pnom Penh ritually took itself to a celebrated pleasure house. The choice was between the dreamy consolation of opium and the delectation of nubile girls (or of young boys), until it was time to return to one's bungalow and change for a dinner party where the talk drifted from news of a recent Malraux raid on a Khmer site to Simone de Beauvoir's latest pronouncement at Louise de Vilmorin's salon in Paris.

At dawn on December 10, we cross the Kwai in the dugout, nudging aside puffs of mist hovering above the surface. A Mon guard is asleep in the Land Rover, parked under the trees on the opposite shore. Jacques is going to drive us to Tha-Khanun. From there on, Aung Song and I will be on our own.

The track leads through a corridor of bamboo marked in places by more substantial trees – teak, rosewood and kapok. Around inhabited areas the jungle has been levelled for the cultivation of cotton and banana. The insidious, floury dust appears wherever topsoil has been irretrievably destroyed. It's only some ten years ago that the tribals started moving into the Kwai valley. Not much time, you would think, to kill the jungle, their only modern tool being power-saws. But in combination with the traditional slash-and-burn method of clearance, they achieved it. The Forestry people have already started to take steps to save the thin topsoil. Teak seedlings are put down, but no sooner are the saplings worth cutting down for charcoal than they disappear at night.

Illegal logging, landless farmers, nomadic hill tribes, road and dam construction, and the gathering of firewood – the main source of fuel – are fast destroying Thailand's forests. In 1963, they covered 51 per cent of the country. By 1978, satellites revealed that the proportion had been reduced to twenty per cent

At the Tha-Khanun ferry we take our turn in line behind bullock-carts, trucks and buses. An hour later we roll on to a creaky bamboo platform lashed to fifty-gallon oildrums. We share the ferry with a minibus of young monks: their hairless brown skins, shaven heads and yellow robes give them a clone look.

A steel cable reaching from shore to shore and a diesel winch haul the contraption across the river. Jacques jokes with the Thai operator, who has the emaciated body of a drug user. He nets daily the equivalent of U.S. $200, and nightly loses it gambling. Upstream, unfortunately for him, elephants are moving logs into position for a bridge which will put him out of business.

A hydro-electric dam due to become operative in a couple of years is under construction north of Tha-Khanun which has now a distinct Wild West flavour. The centre of social life is a cinema fronted by a handpainted canvas of huge dimensions encapsulating the more spectacular scenes of the movie on the programme, in this case a python crushing a Land Rover, bosomy beauties in evening gowns and a gun-toting Siamese version of Jimmy Dean. Life goes some way towards imitating art: in the streets of this ramshackle assemblage of huts, garages, sheds and tents, men carry shotguns and rifles. Hard-hat construction workers drive their trucks recklessly, a couple of girls squeezed next to them in the cab.

The local *jeunesse dorée* rushes around in decorated jeeps, tiger on port side, dragon on starboard, with a rifle rack in the rear and a searchlight mounted above the windscreen. Nightly, they drive into the forest, blind any animal they encounter and blaze away at it. In a bar, over a beer, I ask a couple of these boys, dressed in tight jeans and purple blousons, why. They answer, talking all together with much vehemence and at great length. Aung Song translates succinctly. "They say here nothing to do."

We spend the night in a Mon house. Dinner consists of tofu and vegetable soup, rice and pork, fried bananas and beer. Before turning in, I read over in my P.O.W. diary the pages describing the night marches to Tha-Khanun.

(1943)

On the march from Kinsaiyok, the two Koreans who escorted us gave in to panic, certain we'd lost our way. This was very unlikely, but night and the forest gave rise to strange chimera: the path could have forked out into a game trail; we might never extricate ourselves from the rain-dripping jungle. The Koreans vented their fear by hitting prisoners and using their rifle butts indiscriminately.

The same thoughts drifted in and out of our heads: suppose we overwhelm and kill the two guards, what next? Is it worth struggling further? Why not give up here and now, lie down in the jungle and wait for death? What more of my belongings can I throw away to lighten my load?

The road was an old elephant path, widened into a dry-weather track. With the coming of monsoon it had become a mud stream in which you sank halfway to your knees. The slime oozed into your boots, and pulled them off your feet. In the darkness they were lost for ever.

Man-eating tigers followed us. They were bold. I once saw the glint of eyes burning through thickets a mere ten yards away. The eyes were immobile, watching me. But tigers only attacked men who were isolated from the column. Not even the rain could expunge their smell. Incongruously, it made me think of the Paris *pissotières,* the pungent and acrid *Vespasiennes.* Whenever we stopped we lit fires and crouched around the flames for protection.

Our Koreans were terrified. They melted into the column, making sure there was plenty of potential British or Australian tiger food all around them.

That night, hour after hour, heading the column, a piper from the Argyll & Sutherland Highlanders, played a dirge, inexplicably tender, infinitely sad. The thin, slow sound often waned, drowned out by the beat of the downpour, but always came back like a distant beacon in a storm.

The sky turned a dirty, streaky yellow, and by the light of dawn we crossed a half completed bridge over a small river. Australian P.O.W.s and Burmese coolies were consolidating the pilings, which threatened to wash away.

At Wanping (Kui Ye) we were dumped in a bowl-shaped clearing by the bridge. The trees had been cut down and all that remained were a few bushes half-flattened by wind and rain.

We stayed in that dismal place a ravenous forty-eight hours. The rations were down to a little rice and a few strands of salt fish once a day. R. and I went foraging for building materials, and put up an elaborate lean-to set on a bamboo platform to insulate ourselves from mud and water. The local Japs, notes the diary, "were helpful and sympathetic, but unable to provide anything but words."

On the morning of May 27 the weather cleared and we left Wanping. Once more, we picked up additional sick men who had been left behind. It was a pleasant march: our kits dried in the sun and got lighter; the country was more varied, the road followed mostly a cliff overlooking the river, and beyond it, on our left, we could see the line of hills that separate Burma and Siam.

At midday we halted by a small Japanese camp on the river. We received the usual cup of hot water; we ate our haversack rations – a ball of cooked rice and a pickled plum, what we called "Tea and refreshments". Then, with their inexplicable and sudden urge to please us, the guards took us to the local hot springs. The water came out of the river bed at different temperatures, and had been channelled into three pools. The effect was incredibly invigorating.

Prang Kassi, the next staging area, was a hutted encampment set in the forest on the river bank.

There, we were met by four Japanese armed with sticks. Blows fell on us without reason, punctuated by the usual soundtrack of insults and curses. The leader was a huge Imperial Guards corporal, booted, Hitler-moustached, and perfumed.

At the double (blows raining on heads, backs and legs), we were herded into a compound absolutely barren except for a few dead trees. Once we were properly lined up, we received an excellent stew. We had to finish it in fifteen minutes, after which everyone was detailed to fatigues designed to make the Japanese more comfortable.

We left "Hitler's Camp" with bitterness; we'd had to sleep in the open (no banana and no bamboo), within sight of fifty vacant tents just across the compound.

The monsoon's great opening was over, and now the rain came down relentlessly and monotonously. We switched from a natural habitat of air to one of water. Mud liquefied into thin ooze. Streams overflowed their banks and had to be waded. Feet rotted. Dysentery dissolved our bowels and our skin was chafed raw.

Even the stretches of road where thousands of saplings had been laid down to form a "washboard" became impassable to motor traffic. The Japanese were now organising elephant convoys.

The column strung out even further than usual. When the Koreans were dealing brutally with a straggler the word would filter up front, where I was generally to be found, that I'd better go back "and calm down a Nip going round the bend". Eventually, I took my place with the rearguard.

At Tha-Khanun, the reception committee consisted of one man, a short and wiry Japanese wearing white gloves. With a bamboo he hit the head and shoulders of anyone not strictly in line. We went through a gap in a fence and joined some thirty head of cattle wallowing in a waterlogged field of mud and grass. Half a pint of rice, with a pinch of salt, was ladled out. From now on we were to be on half rations. Our white-gloved friend distributed additional biffs to the prisoners whose attitude didn't please him. But for those he approved of there was extra rice. To be on his good list you held your head high, you moved smartly and you looked straight in front of you – the perfect little soldier.

I obtained permission for anyone to leave the field and gather building materials: we were going to spend at least a couple of days in Tha-Khanun.

Inexplicably, my previous building companion, Major R., has disappeared from the diary, and has been replaced by O.M., a rubber planter. Together, we built our shelter.

The distractions of Tha-Khanun must have worn thin on the Japanese. Learning there was someone who spoke their language among the new arrivals, they visited me in the lean-to. The conversation opened generally with a request to view the obscene postcards that all Westerners, as is well known, carry on their person.

To punish us for our omission, we had to listen to tales of the prowess of the I.J.A. We heard that the Imperial Marines had marched through the streets of London after a successful landing on the Thames Estuary.

I said, trying to look amazed and appalled, *"Ah so desu ka? Honto desu ka?"* – is it so, is it true? – while O.M. for whom I translated the news, gave his own opinion: "No importance at all. It's the last battle that counts."

"And who is going to win it?" asked our visitor, a terribly young *nitto-hei*, a second class private.

"Eikoku to Beikoku!" I quickly answered, "England and America!", not knowing the compound for "the Allies". To O.M. (and to me) the two words sounded faintly unserious for

our geopolitical exchange, more suitable as the names of two Japanese comics.

"What on earth did you say just now?" O.M wanted to know. I explained. "Yes, that's it," shouted O.M., "Kokukokukoku!"

Nitto-hei looked worried. "Perhaps you are right," he said, "but don't say that to other Nippon soldiers. They are not like me." He gave us a pack of cigarettes and left.

We left Tha-Khanun at eight in the evening, after packing our kits and pulling down the shelters (we couldn't possibly abandon our bits of string or cloth). We lined up, numbered off and the Japanese escort announced they would wait for the weather to clear. Chilled to the bone, we built fires and hung around until one in the morning.

From the start of the march we were stiff and in poor spirit. The guards imagined they were lost and started hitting the men at the rear as a way of unloading their anxiety. As the sun rose we saw the river. The haze was tinged a vivid pink, and the hills in the west were touched with flaming orange. In its eddies and rapids, the ochre river scintillated pink and orange.

We crossed groups of prisoners building a ledge for the railway track along a steep escarpment. They were naked except for a loincloth, and barefoot. They had arrived in Thailand, they told us, six months before.

The road veered off the river bank and plunged back into the forest. Lianas the size of a man's thigh wove through the thickets of bamboo and the boles of deciduous trees arcing above them. Small orchids nestled in the fern undergrowth. Although we had been told we would see them, of tigers and elephants there was no trace. Either the forest was impenetrable even to them, or more likely they kept away from the track and the foulness of man.

A company of Japanese infantry overtook us, making their way to Burma on foot, at twice our speed. Their captain was holding his sword above his head, attempting to keep it dry, in a parody of surrender. His men were as bedraggled and filthy as we were. Fifty were harnessed to a cart loaded with heavy equipment. The cart foundered in ruts and sank in mud pools. As they went by, I said, "*Taihen, desu ne?* Bloody awful, isn't it?" They looked through me, surprised, perhaps disgusted that I'd pass such a remark. I'll never know. But the Japanese never expect a *gaijin*, a foreigner, to speak their language, and when he does, often they're unsure of what they have heard.

These troops had boots; they weren't sick and they didn't go hungry. But our men said, "Better be a prisoner of the Nips than be in the Nip army."

At noon we stopped outside a village laid out in the shade of betel palms. Three or four houses had been burned to the ground. We soon found out why: notices in Japanese warned of cholera. From the village a track led west across the hills to the lower reaches of Burma.

The rain forest closed in, dank and opaque, and we slipped into a leaden lethargy. At times the reek of death impregnated the vaporous air, as we trudged by the carcasses of bullocks disintegrating by the side of their abandoned carts; or the bodies of coolies, lying crumpled beneath a rice-sack. Green flies left their carrion and swarmed around us, competing with the clouds of gnats feeding on our faces.

We'd been on the go for thirteen hours, and my hold on life was weakening. For days I'd been passing bloody stools, and now I was shivering with a bout of malaria.

I had a distinct image of a web that tied my "I", the indivisible consciousness of myself, to a vast, inchoate yet perceptible "non I". The strands of the web were becoming blurred. I sank into an autistic state, aware of moving one leg, then another; and of a mortal pain buried deep in the gut.

As we were going through a dark and convoluted part of the jungle, I slunk away, hid, and when the last of the column was out of sight, laid myself down on a bed of ferns, waiting for death.

Lying on my back, eyes closed, I felt a presence. It was a Thai balancing a bunch of bananas on his head. I opened my pack, offered him a pair of khaki shorts, and mimed putting food in my mouth. The Thai deposited the bananas by my side, took the shorts and went off in the direction of the cholera village. I devoured the whole bunch, a dozen or more bananas. I stood up, and a tremendous fart exploded, breaking the stillness of the forest, almost knocking me down. The gut untwisted, and I felt life flowing once again. For an hour, until I reached Tamuron Part I walked effortlessly. I found everyone collapsed on the ground: I could imagine the guards giving the order to stop and, overcome by gravity, bodies dropping *sur place*. No one, apparently, had missed me.

Cameron Park (to use its P.O.W. transliteration) was a small Japanese tented camp, in effect an incongruous park for about eighty trucks immobilised by the monsoon and the impassable road. Bamboo and banana leaves were abundant; the Japanese were helpful; the rations improved, and from Thai traders who came up the river by raft we bought tobacco. After four days in Tamuron Part I felt a lot better.

Two men died of dysentery, and we buried them in the jungle. The cholera rumours became cholera news, and one morning Japanese medical orderlies arrived on foot to administer prophylactic injections, using tremendous horse syringes that they never either changed or cleaned.

(1979)

The Land Rover went into a repair shop at Tha-Khanun, but as it's ready sooner than expected, Jacques says he'll drive us all the way to Sangkla Buri.

We stop at the village of Wang Patho which, according to the map, must have been Tamuron Part. The general store is also the headman's house. Jacques has heard that up river there should be a wrecked train. We start negotiations with the headman to hire a couple of boats.

Aung Song tells the villagers why we are here, and who I am. I'm suddenly surrounded. I'm felt, stroked, pinched, and examined. My limbs are seized as if they were not attached to my body, and passed from hand to hand to be appraised. Clearly, everyone's amazed. Aung Song explains: they can't believe I'm still alive. "He must be terribly strong," say the women. "All the same he shouldn't be around after all this time," say the men. The children gawk. I'm transformed into the sole survivor of a species long thought extinct, a living exhibit fit for a natural history museum, or better, a zoo.

Wang Patho with its two rice mills (crude, foot-actuated pounders) is a trading centre for the neighbouring villages. Its 650 inhabitants live in 110 houses. The chief building material is fashioned from the fronds of the Nipa palm, and every year, at the most every two years, the houses have to be rebuilt. An air of impermanence hangs over the region. The Karens, roughly half the population, go in for what is known as "shifting cultivation", growing mainly upland rice. These Burmese Karens are classified as 'landless people', but this is an unfair label as some of them have been in the area for two generations. (At the time the Japanese started pushing the railway through, there were only a few families settled here, but they left, fearing both cholera and the invaders.)

Jacques and I climb into a dugout propelled by a small outboard engine. An old man with a shotgun sits in the stern next to the boatman: Communist guerillas, he tells us with aplomb, have been spotted on the Great Kwai (we're on the smaller arm) and the headman, conscious of his responsibility, wants to make sure we're well protected.

We put-put upstream for half an hour. Blue kingfishers and long-tailed magpies skim over the clear water. Traces of man are scarce: a bamboo fishtrap or a raft tied to the bank. We approach the rapids and step ashore to lighten the boat: the engine's full power will be needed to negotiate the rush of water. When we re-embark, a mile further up, a second man armed with a .22 rifle pulls his craft up to ours. We are to travel together.

By six we land on a small beach and wade 150 yards along a creek. The blue dusk slowly envelops us. We're stopped short by a tangle of broken and blackened bamboo arching over three boxcars heaped helterskelter on the flank of the ravine. Above, lianas weave an aerial net. Swooping down, they wrap the wreckage in their tentacles. In the bed of the creek itself, among the broken concrete piles of the bridge, two more wagons lie on their side, torn and gnawed by rust. At our approach, a *pointilliste* cloud of bats and flying foxes shoots out of the doors of the boxcars, streams down the ravine, ascends through the trees and, like smoke, evaporates. A monkey screams.

The light is fast fading but the inscription on the wheels – Federated Malay States Railways – is still visible. Colour leaches out of the forest. Fireflies dart around the wagons. I smell ghosts here. For the first time since I sat by the bridge at Kanchanaburi, feeling nothing, I am sad, terribly sad.

Night falls. Venus makes a luminous hole in the darkening sky, then Orion defines itself. On the shore, the small fires of fishermen flicker, and the smell of woodsmoke spreads across the

The Selarang Barrack Square incident. This photograph was taken by George Aspinall, an Australian from F Force, using x-ray film which he cut up and inserted into a 6 × 9 cm rollfilm camera. Not only did he take his camera up-country, he managed to process the film on the spot. Aspinall's caption reads: '15,400 British and Australian troops were herded into an area which usually held 1,200, I took eight shots from the A.I.F. building – some from behind the parapet seen in the bottom right-hand corner.' (This photograph and four others are taken from *Changi Photographer*, by George Aspinall and Tim Bowden, courtesy of the Australian Broadcasting Corporation. All other photographs, except as noted, are by the author.)

(above) *F Force assembling for the Burma Railway* (Aspinall/Bowden)

(below) *The Wampo viaducts, built by P.O.W.s* (1979)

The wrecked train at Wan Patho (1979)

(*above*) *Jacques Bes's river rafts at Kinsaiyok* (1979)

(*below*) *The bridge at Sangkla Buri* (1979)

(*above*) *The Tha-Khanun ferry*

(*below*) *The road and railway bridge at Sonkurai, 1943*
(author's sketch on roll-call form)

(above) *Cholera Hill, Shimo Sonkurai No. 1 Camp* (Aspinall/Bowden).
Aspinall: 'This photograph brings back many traumatic memories ... Cholera
patients were housed under canvas on the left of the photo. In the centre is the
operating table used for amputations, ulcer treatment and post-mortems. A
mosquito net was hung over the crossbar above the table to try to keep the blowflies
away. The box on the table contains what surgical instruments were available. If
someone died, the body was carried on a bamboo stretcher (there is one to the
right of the hospital tent) over to the small holding tent on the right. Later the
bodies were burned in the area towards the back right-hand side of the picture ...
I think it is quite remarkable that there is so much detail, I was using coarse-grained
x-ray material at this stage, and my developing chemicals were becoming weak
through much use'

(above right) *The burning of the cholera dead: drawing by Charles Thrale in 'Indian
ink on packing cardboard obtained from a Thai'* (Imperial War Museum). The
caption reads: 'These men died in a hospital near No. 2 camp (Sonkurai). Some
escaped to get to the river to drink. They died on the bank, and many dead bodies
floated down the river to spread the infection to other camps. Parties of prisoners
were sent to collect them. Our taskmasters were scared stiff of any disease, and
left the cholera ward strictly alone. It was the only place one could be sure of not
seeing them, and some natives volunteered to work among the cholera patients in
order to get away from the Japs. Very few who entered the hospital came out alive.
Bodies were burned as opposed to burial because they were afraid the infection
would seep through the soil to infect their drinking water. It was a quick death –
very few lived longer than 48 hours after the infection'

(right) *Three 'fit'*
workers at Shimo
Sonkurai No. 1 Camp
(Aspinall/Bowden).
Aspinall: 'The
Japanese considered
these men fit for
work. The man on the
right can't do his
shorts up because
his stomach is
swollen with beri-
beri. Ossie Jackson
(centre) has wet
beri-beri in his
legs, which are
virtually the same
diameter from his
ankles up to his
thighs. Benjamin
Pearce (left) is
also suffering
from malnutrition
and beri-beri'

(above) *The Three Pagodas on the Thai-Burma border (1979)*

(below) *The village at the Three Pagodas Pass (1979)*

(above) *Villagers preparing for the dances at the Three Pagodas Pass* (1979)

(below) *The dances* (1979)

(above) *General Nai Schwe Kyin and Mon cabinet ministers (1979)*

(below) *The bridge at Apalon; author in the water (1979)*

(right) *The Reverend Ottama at the Sangkla Buri monastery (1979)*

(below) *The last photograph: Two troop trains, Kanchanaburi, Thailand (Aspinall/Bowden). Aspinall: 'You could always tell Australians on the move by the billycans about the place. We were on our way back to Singapore ... Unfortunately the searches by the Japanese military police, the* Kempei Tai, *became so tough that I had to destroy my camera shortly after this photo was taken'*

The author back in Singapore, February 1944. (Sketch by Charles Thrale in Changi)

river. We cut the engine and shoot the rapids. The other boat loses its propeller and we take it in tow.

Back at Wang Patho we sit around a fire. After a fish curry, we're led to an empty room in one of the village houses. Straw pallets and thin, exeedingly dubious-looking blankets are brought in. We spend the night fighting mosquitoes and squashing bedbugs.

When morning comes, we're taken to view a couple of tumuli half a mile from the village. Buried below, the villagers say, lie gold, silver and jewellery stolen by the Japanese. No one has dared dig them up; they are certainly booby-trapped. I don't say anything. They are merely prisoners' graves.

(1943)

Two more days were needed to reach the base camps – two days which summed up the pain of the march.

On June 3, we left at first light, under the command of a Japanese officer. The column immediately unravelled, with men strung out singly or in tiny groups, making slow headway. Not only had the four-day rest softened us, but the track had vanished under a substance that, perversely, combined both viscosity and adherence.

Alternately we used threats and encouragements to urge on the men who were weakening. In the last extremity we carried them, taking our turns on the stretchers, along with our six-gallon cooking pots, shovels, medical supplies and sodden kits.

It was good to have one friend, a "mate", who cared for you; for whom your disappearance would cause not only grief but also be the harbinger of his own death. Such was the nature of the bond found in the two-man unit, and the secret of its strength: one man's survival rested on the other. On these last stages of the march, it was clear that the group's ability to provide protection and support was dangerously eroded.

By midnight, we were only two-thirds of the way to our destination. We'd been marching for fifteen hours on half a pint of rice. In the far distance, an electrical storm was raging. The unceasing downpour drowned its rumble, but the black and monstrous bio-mass of vegetation through which we were advancing was rent by streaks of silent lightning. We shivered with cold, and were gripped by archaic fears.

We were close to Konkuita, and orders were received to halt and await instructions. I laid myself down in the mud, pulling a corner of my groundsheet over my head, and went to sleep.

At one a.m. we were roused by an Australian who led us to a cookhouse by the river, a mile further on. We passed under a railway bridge gaunt and ghostly in the night, standing in surrealist isolation, issuing from nowhere, leading nowhere. We lit fires, waiting for the rice to be cooked. At three a.m. we were fed. But cholera had broken out in the vicinity, and we were ordered to be off. I objected but lost. Three miles further on, we were allowed to flop down in a jungle clearing, a place where, like salmon in the Sargasso Sea, all the sand-flies of South-East Asia must have returned to breed.

Shortly after dawn I was roused by a boot in the ribs. Close by, but invisible in the dark, stood three tents occupied by Japanese Engineers. The booted foot belonged to the corporal in charge.

"You're not allowed near us," he shouted. "Don't you know that?" Prisoners and coolies were already synonymous with cholera. I told him, no, I didn't know, this was the first time in my life I'd visited his little camp. The consequence of my irony, such as it was, was instantly felt in the form of a couple of cracks on the ear.

We were told to erect our shelters half a mile further on. No one on the Kwai would ever forget Konkuita, the 262-kilo mark: it was here that cholera had first broken out among the coolies, and here that the prisoners picked it up after sheltering in their heavily contaminated huts. It was also three kilometres further north that six months later, in October, the junction would be made between the railway track that originated in Burma and the line that came up north from Banpong.

O.M. was sick. Single-handed I built the lean-to, gathered wood for the fire and collected our rations – a ladle of mouldy, unsalted rice – at a cookhouse reached at the end of a mile-long slithery path. Although I wasn't feverish any more my stools were still thickly laced with blood, and I was weaker than ever since leaving Banpong.

Of our group, five men were so obviously ill that they would never be unable to resume the march the following day. We debated what to do with them: we were loath to leave them behind and loath to carry them.

Making matters worse, the Japanese stuck on us three men from the cookhouse at Konkuita; bloated as they were with oedematous beri-beri, they stood an excellent chance of dropping dead with heart failure as soon as they got on their way. A cookhouse job was certainly no guarantee of survival. White (or polished) rice contains hardly anything more than carbohydrates and trace minerals. In order to assimilate it, the body needed to draw on its reserves of vitamin B, so that in the absence of any other foods, the more rice you eat the more likely you are to suffer from beri-beri. Clearly, the eight very sick men would have to be carried on improvised stretchers. The Japanese allowed us, reasonably for once to abandon them at Upper Konkuita, four miles away, a work camp manned by Australians who would care for them.

It took us four hours to cover the distance. The Japanese officer ordered the guards to beat the sick if they did not advance fast enough to please him, and he made me translate the order so that everyone knew what was in store. When we reached Kong Kwoita, we touched despair: the camp was in the process of evacuation. As no food could reach it any more from the Siam side it was being moved further north where, it was hoped, supplies would be brought down from Burma. The sick would have to be carried further.

We were soon engulfed in the flow of prisoners, coolies and bullock carts moving out of the camp. The Japanese were orchestrating the exodus with their usual brutality.

The track led across a wooden bridge that spanned the river, then snaked up the opposite bank, and disappeared into the jungle. The bridge swayed and threatened to collapse under the press and confusion. The bank had been churned into a small mud avalanche. As we scrambled up the broken slope we went by bullocks still tied to their carts; all that was visible of them was eyes and muzzle emerging from the mud. Sometimes laughing and at others cursing, the Japanese prodded them with bayonets and drove sticks into their flesh. The beasts bellowed, eyes crazed, but remained immobile. The Australians vainly tried to free the carts, straining at the thick wooden spokes in an attempt to force the wheels to turn.

Only twelve miles separated us from the next camp. My diary repetitively relates the usual suffering. However, it had been a short day: we had marched for only eleven hours.

"After following the worst three miles we had yet encountered," I read in the diary, "we arrived towards 7 p.m. at Lower Nikki." This was the base camp for F Force. It was like going home, in a new house perhaps, but we joined our friends, our military family.

And we said, as we had done when we came down the gangplank of the *Mount Vernon,* when we detrained in Banpong, and later when we left the Banpong camp, "Well, thank God for this. Nothing will ever be worse than what we've just been through." Once more, however, we were wrong.

SEVEN

(1979)
By mid-morning the Land Rover stops by the Sangkla Buri bridge over the Kwai.

During the war it was called Lower Nikki. Now, ten years after the "ethnics" started moving up the Kwai basin, it has become the largest settlement in the area. The wooden bridge over the river is a tracery of spindly beams. As if a child with the skill of a spider and a horror of economy had built it on a tiny scale, using matchsticks and glue; then, by an act of magic, had enlarged it and turned it over to the adults for their own use.

It's a footbridge, although a vigorous walk will cause it to sway. But provided the current is sluggish and the water level low, it will support the weight of a bullock cart. The bridge links the Mons on one side of the river with the Thais on the other – 4,000 people in all. The Mons control the country from here right up to the frontier with Burma and the Three Pagodas Pass, But, of course, we are still in Thailand proper.

We lunch at a chop-house by the bridge, and then drive up to a large bungalow hidden in a grove, one of the guerillas' supply depots. Bes is made welcome. Everyone knows him as a friend of the Mons. We're assigned a vast and dark storeroom where we put down our kit, and spread out our sleeping rolls on the wooden floor. Boxes of ammo and weapons are stacked along a wall. Above our sleeping area hangs a framed colour photograph, taken eight years ago, showing the representative of the central government in Rangoon (the celebrated U Nu was then its head), conferring with the Karen, Shan, Mon and Arakan chiefs to stop the conflict that had started soon after Independence. An accord was never reached, and the internecine war was resumed after a short lull.

An officer points to a padlocked door; it's General Nai Schwe Kyin's own room. A black-and-white photograph showing him in uniform has been nailed above the transom. The general is the Commander-in-Chief and Chairman of the New Mon State. Aung Song thinks it proper that I write him a note, saying who I am and why I'm travelling in the area. I also ask permission to visit him. Aung Song delivers the letter to a house in Sangkla Buri and assures me that a messenger will take it to the Chairman.

The following morning, as we're back at our eating-place by the bridge, we meet an old Thai who says that he came here in 1945, riding his elephant, and that he used to sell fruit to the Japanese.

"There were only about a hundred prisoners left," he explains, "and when the English planes appeared, the Japanese ordered all the English prisoners on to the bridge, so the people flying the planes would see them and not bomb the bridge." The bridge in question was a mile north of where we are sitting, spanning a tributary of the Kwai. This story is completely new to me, but it's probably apocryphal.

Jacques wishes us good luck, and turns the Land Rover around: he's returning to his rafts. We're staying on, as Aung Song has arranged an audience with the abbot of the local monastery. If the Mon National Army of Liberation, the M.N.L.A., is the military and executive branch of government, the Reverend Ottama is both the spiritual and legislative master of the region. His temporal power is such that, Mon émigré though he is, he can call on a Thai Army helicopter to transport him to his distant parishes, or to Bangkok. In Sangkla Buri itself, he has imposed an alcohol and prostitution ban on both Thais and Mons.

The new monastery, the new *wat*, is suitably *nouveau riche*, yellow, white and gold with polychrome stained glass windows. If the Thais had wedding cakes, it would serve admirably as an oversized prototype.

The Reverend Ottama is seated on a blue silk cushion in the centre of the great hall, a bulk of rust-red cloth from which the head emerges, round, bare, shaven. The face is fleshy, the features coarse, and the eyes remain permanently half-closed, as if in meditation.

The Reverend's colour portrait, blown-up three feet tall, is hung high on every one of the six columns that hold up the *wat's* roof.

I bow deeply, and as I've been instructed, I fold my legs beneath me, and tuck my feet away from the abbot.

The question is asked: What am I doing here? While he's listening to Aung Song, the Rev. clears his throat and directs a large gob into a spitoon embellished with gaudy decals. He turns to a young bespectacled monk sitting on the floor next to him. After a few whisperings, the Rev. hands me a small red copper medal: on one side it carries his effigy; on the other Phra Chedi, the Three Pagodas.

Aung Song is amazed. Receiving such a talisman is exceptional: any Bangkok jeweller would buy it from me for the equivalent of U.S. $20.

We climb in the back of a truck going to the border, and join a dozen locals, mainly Mon soldiers and farmers. Everyone has found his perch or his niche among the sacks of rice, the baskets of vegetables, and the boxes of canned goods. For a seat, I spread out my bedroll on crates of Fanta, Thailand's favourite pop drink. A young Burmese who speaks some English asks if he can share my improvised bench. He explains that he has studied "commerce" in Bangkok, and that he's returning to Thanbyuzayat, his home town.

The road is the old Japanese track, unimproved, rutty, bumpy, and washed out every monsoon season. We hang on to whatever we can grab, and jerk up and down like dislocated puppets. I'm hypnotised by the logo and shield of Princeton University jiggling right in front of me. Imprinted on a white t-shirt they cover beautiful breasts – high, firm and, like everything else in the truck, mobile. The breasts are only one of the assets of the driver's young wife, who smiles provocatively at me, exhibiting the whitest, sharpest and most regular teeth of anyone south of the Burma border. I'm smitten. Through Aung Song I learn that she has never been to Princeton, that the beauty doesn't even know where or what Princeton is, and that she bought the t-shirt in Tha-Khanun. Everyone laughs: my lusting is evident but nothing will come of it with husband and his M-16 carbine sitting in the cab.

No "ethnics" have settled in this stretch of jungle; no signs of slash-and-burn, even of tree cutting. For the first time I sense a profound, even a disturbing familiarity with my surrounding.

We have left the Kwai proper. We ford the Mae Nam Ranti, one of the several feeders to the Kwai's catchment area.

The truck lurches slowly along the road to Sonkurai.

(1943)

Before we had even reached Lower Nikki, Colonel Harris, last seen leaving Kanyu alone on top of a Marmon truck, came to greet us. Our ultimate destination was Nikki proper, he said, only two miles across the river, and if we wanted to we could go there straight away. Nikki was the main base for the seven camps of F Force, dispersed over a seventeen mile stretch all the way to the Three Pagodas Pass.

We didn't. Tonight better go and sleep in huts, even leaky huts, and eat a hot meal of rice, meat and onions.

Lower, or Shimo Nikki, where we were spending the night was the southernmost of the working camps alloted to F Force. But it was about to be shut down: cholera had broken out, a dozen men had been buried and many more were expected to die; the river was in flood, the road bridge had washed away and no supplies could be expected for a long time. The evacuation across the river was to take place only forty-eight hours hence.

We were shown to an atap hut standing in a waterlogged field. The Thai and Indian coolies' lines sprawled out further down; and by the river, stood the hutments of the Japanese Engineers and the guards.

The British and Australian prisoners in Nikki proper numbered around six hundred. They were a disparate lot, too sick or too weak to keep up with the columns. Belonging to different units, separated from their officers and N.C.O.s, they were, to use the strange expression of the times, a "shower". Discipline had withered. Elementary notions of solidarity and mutual help had largely vanished. Survival was equated with theft.

Colonel F.J.Dillon, Indian Army, was in charge of Nikki. In Changi we had heard his story, and he was a much admired officer: ordered to leave Singapore a few days before surrender, he had reached Sumatra where, instead of racing ahead to safety, he had organised other escape parties trying to make for Ceylon. But this had cost him his freedom. He had been recaptured and sent to Changi.

Until Major Wild's arrival from Lower Nikki, I was camp interpreter. Dillon called for me; he wanted to address the men after roll-call, and the Japanese would have to be warned. But what he had to say was not for their ears. I was to try and get them to leave the moment the men had been counted.

Roll-call over, I saw with relief the Japanese return to their quarters. The prisoners were waiting in untidy rows of fours, expecting to be dismissed.

Dillon stood straight, feet apart, and faced them.

"Dogs!" he said as if all the breath was being expelled from his lungs. "You complain of being treated like dogs by your own officers! Well, it may be so, but I didn't imagine that British soldiers could behave the way you do. Yes, you'll probably say the Japs are responsible. But I'll let you have it straight out: I've never seen such scum of the earth as I see here assembled in Nikki. I never thought that such scoundrels could come out of England. And I hate to think that I deliberately sacrificed my freedom in Sumatra for the likes of you!"

Then came the reason he wanted the Japanese out of the way. His voice rose.

"Now, you tell me, are we going to let these bastards think that the white man, even in defeat, behaves like an animal?"

The prisoners stood immobile, murmuring. For a moment, I thought they were going to break rank and attack Dillon. I was wrong. The murmur signified admiration. Dillon thanked them. But his voice wavered. He was close to tears.

Dillon stood up to the Japanese. Colonel Banno, inspecting the hospital huts, remarked on "the disgraceful way" those prisoners who still had boots had cut them. The reason, Dillon answered, coldly angry, was the inhumanity of the guards who drove the prisoners regardless of the suppurating wounds on their feet. Of course the prisoners looked filthy and unmilitary. How could it be otherwise? At the end of a night's march, the guards found shelter and good food; and they never had to cover more than twenty miles a week. How could they be compared to us? I translated, and Banno went quiet.

There were so few fit men at Nikki that work on the railway line and the embankments stopped. A small party left the camp every day simply to try and maintain the road. A hundred men in hospital were not expected to recover. The cemetery was growing in size. A month previously a dozen prisoners had been sent from Lower Nikki to try and save the bridge. For twelve hours a day they worked in the river, with water chest-high. Now they were all dead.

Yet the reports coming through from the other camps were worse. So when on June 9 a Korean whom I had known in Changi came down from Sonkurai, the main British camp, specifically to ask for my transfer there, I begged him not to paint too dark a picture to Colonel Banno. But he told me (this was exceptional and deeply worrying as Koreans and Japanese always presented a rosy picture of any situation) that Sonkurai was *taihen*, bloody terrible. Cholera was sweeping through the camp; the Engineers were savage; and the rations desperately scant.

I'd only been four days in Nikki, and Cyril Wild was expected at any moment. I was ordered to leave: perhaps a Japanese speaker would help solve some of the problems. Colonel Banno saw me off. He ordered my escort of two Koreans to carry all my kit and take good care of me. I saluted him, and he wished me a good journey.

We walked in a leisurely way to Shimo (Lower) Sonkurai, the main Australian camp of F Force, which we reached in time for *meshi*, the Japanese word for rice which up and down the line had replaced all the ways English has to describe food and meals. *Meshi* was well prepared but not as plentiful as at Nikki. The camp was neatly kept, the latrines covered, and sanitation well enforced. But the deaths from cholera and dysentery were already in three figures. The burial ground was a hill well beyond the camp site.

It was another three miles to Sonkurai, where I arrived with my two Koreans laden with my gear. I hoped that the panache of my arrival with my two Korean bearers was not lost on the Engineers. I probably needed all the status I could get.

The camp was laid out just beyond the river (not the Kwai but the Huai Ro Khi), and spread out on both sides of the road. I could see eight very large atap huts, each about a hundred feet long. Six were used by prisoners only, but two on the opposite side of the road from the river were shared with Burmese coolies. The cookhouse itself stood on the river bank.

I was taken to my hut, on the slope of a hill. Like all the others, it was falling apart, the walls swayed to one side, and the rain seeped through the atap roof. So few fit men were available for camp duties, I was told, that no repairs could ever be made. Yet the Korean guards lived at one end; at the other, our officers; and in the centre, the senior N.C.O.s.

Colonel Hingston, who was in charge, explained the different problems that affected our relations with the Japanese. He also described what they found when the main parties started arriving three weeks ago. The huts had not been completed; the only one with a roof was taken over by the Japanese and our officers; there wasn't even a cookhouse. Everything remained to be done. Yet orders were received that the following morning ninety per cent of the men were required to parade for work, leaving a bare few to take care of the sick and prepare food. All possibility of improving the living quarters was excluded.

The conditions were dismal. It was forbidden to light fires inside the huts, and the monsoon rain kept coming down. Everyone was permanently wet and shivering with cold.

Two days after the first columns reached the camp, cholera broke out. Scores of men were instantly affected. They were isolated in a specific part of the camp, but on the second night, in the middle of a storm, the Japanese Engineers ordered them removed without delay and deposited up the hill, half a mile from the camp. The order was seen as a deliberate killing of the cholera patients (presumably to save the working force) by denying them shelter. In the darkness, in spite of high winds and lashing rain, two or three leaky tents were set up. At first light, however, a dreadful thing was revealed: the cholera hill had been the coolies' cremation area. Half consumed bodies were strewn about, rotting in the rain and the mud, covered in flies.

The worst days of the march, said Hingston, were nothing compared to the sufferings of the last three weeks.

(1979)
The truck stops as the road dips down a river bank – the Huai Ro Khi. But this can't be Sonkurai; of the three-span wooden trestle bridge, all that's left is a couple of wooden stakes emerging from the water. There must be a mistake. No one in the trucks knows

for certain. I walk around, looking for traces. Aung Song calls: we must be on our way.

(1943)

"No work, no *meshi*," was the rule in Sonkurai. The Engineers' reasoning was simple: survival depended on keeping the road open for food supplies to reach us. Anyone who failed to contribute to this collective task didn't get fed.

As in Nikki, embankment and bridge construction had been stopped. When I got there, of the 1600 who had arrived three weeks previously, only 300 were fit for work. If their rations, already at subsistence level, had to be shared with the sick, everyone would be dead of starvation within a few days. In effect, the sick were at most times issued with half-rations, not enough to survive on, so a portion, but not half, of the working men's rice was diverted to them.

The senior Engineer officer was Lieutenant Abe. Relations with him had been tolerably good at the beginning when Lieutenant Colonels Pope and Ferguson had been in charge. They deteriorated after both officers fell ill, and been replaced by Lieutenant Colonel Hingston.

Abe disliked Hingston. He found him a lot tougher than his predecessors. Fences had to be mended. A couple of men in Sonkurai knew a few words of Japanese and were useful on the working sites, but any sustained discussion was beyond them. The sergeant in charge of our Koreans, *"Honcho dono"* or "Mister Master" as he instructed me to call him, sided with us whenever he could. Confronted with the Engineers, he was as powerless as we were.

Hingston and I went to see Abe the day I got in. We were going to try and get him to agree that a number of fit men be held back from the road parties, and made available for heavy camp duties.

We drew up a list of those needed in camp, the medical orderlies and the cooks; men to dig latrines; and men to cut wood for the cookhouse, the funeral pyres and the fires inside the huts. We haggled. Abe agreed to the figure of 120, leaving 200 to work on the road.

That evening, our N.C.O.s called out the names for the road gang, and those whose duties would keep them in camp.

The day started always at six a.m., in darkness. The fires in the aisle were down to embers. We woke to the sound of the rain seeping through the leaky atap roof and trickling down to the soggy ground; to the moaning of the sick and the obscenities of the fit dragging themselves out of their sleep and their dreams. We revived the fires, filled our mess-tins with water and brewed old tea leaves. *Meshi* was watery rice which we called pap; sometimes a few brown beans were floating in it.

The working parties had to be off by 9 a.m., but two hours earlier they were already lined up in front of the guard-room. One third of those detailed the previous night had gone down sick or were so enfeebled they couldn't drag themselves out of the huts. The men stood hunched under the drizzle, in rags, and mostly barefoot. Dirt coated their limbs. No one spoke. From time to time, a man crumpled up on the ground, unconscious, and was dragged back to his hut. The two hours were needed to find the full complement the Engineers demanded.

I'd been told that unless the required number of working men was supplied, the Engineers entered the huts and dragged out anyone they pleased – however sick – and sent them off to road, bridge or embankment. But on my first morning in Sonkurai, I was certain all would go smoothly: and in conformity with the previous evening's conversation with Abe, we presented two hundred men for road duty. Colonel Hingston, medical officers, the adjutant of the day, and a regimental sergeant major were present.

A squad of Engineers with a corporal in charge took over from the guards. "*Jodan desuka?* Is this a joke?" asked the corporal. "I need three hundred, not two hundred."

I told him what had been agreed with Abe.

"I'm the one who does the work," answered the corporal, "Not Lieutenant Abe. I'm the one who decides on numbers. Get me the other hundred immediately."

I rushed over to Abe's hut.

"Never mind what I told you last night," said Abe. "If my men want three hundred, then that's what they'll have. Go away!"

Cholera, the number one killer at the time, had already caused over two hundred deaths in Sonkurai. The first to go under were men from the Manchester Regiment who, at Changi, had received only half of their prophylatic injections. The speed of the epidemic had been terrifying: every day for the first week, a score of men had died.

At the onset came the "rice-water" stools, followed by vomiting and cramps. Liquids leached out of the body. The chances of survival were one in five: we had no drugs, not even saline solutions to combat dehydration.

The patient was carried to the isolation ward, a hut on the hill. At the entrance, corpses were stacked like logs waiting to be carried to the funeral pyre that burned night and day.

Once inside, he was deposited on a bamboo platform viscous with excrement and vomit. The air was laden with the stench of rot and death. All around him men were dying.

In the space of a few hours a twenty-year-old boy was transformed into a broken, emaciated wreck, sunken into his own body, a mummy of extreme pallor. Few lasted more than a couple of days. The corporal in charge of the cremating party felt the first cramps early morning. By evening his body was in the flames.

As the Japanese feared that their work force might soon be wiped out, they organised teams of medics who, once a month in every camp, carried out tests in order to detect the cholera-carriers. We had a name for it, "bum-stabbing". We formed a line, gave our name and number, and dropped our shorts (or more likely our "jap-happies", the piece of cloth we had fashioned like a *fundoshi*, the traditional Japanese underpants). Docilely, we bent over and a glass rod was pushed up our backsides. Carriers were exiled to the isolation hill where they were put to work. They seldom died of cholera but of the panoply of deadly illnesses (principally dysentery, malaria and tropical ulcers) that was fast depleting Sonkurai.

The river carried the epidemic from villagers to coolies to prisoners, and from camp to camp. But so did the folly of our own men: the cremating party, we found out, was stripping the dead and selling their clothing to the coolies.

We hardened, life and death in Sonkurai made it unavoidable. Sentimentality would have been fatal. Even the Japanese were surprised. One day, after work had been resumed on the bridge, a colonel arrived on an inspection tour. He offered me a cigarette.

Neither of us had the means to light it, but on our left we could see smoke rising from behind a hill.

We arrived at the funeral pyre, always a gruesome sight. A score of bodies were burning. Flesh bubbled, and limbs writhed. I bent down, with one hand protecting my face from the heat, and with the other picking out a burning twig. I held it out to the colonel. He backed away.

"Is that so?" he said. "Is that the way you light your cigarette from the fire that's consuming your friends?"

I replied that life was terrible here, and it was better to face it as it was. I used a Japanese expression, *shikata ga nai koto,* a nothing-to-be-done thing; an inevitability before which it's better to bend. The colonel looked at me, and lit his cigarette from mine.

I thought of the morning a few days back when, observing the man who slept next to me and thinking he wouldn't last the day, I asked him to let me have his toothbrush. As soon as his body was taken out of our hut, his belongings would be looted. And I needed a toothbrush; mine had been stolen.

He said, "Take what you need." He knew that he only had a few hours left. I placed my hand on his shoulder, and said adieu silently. And then opened his pack and took the toothbrush.

There was a dreadful symmetry to our days – in their beginnings and in their endings, in the morning line-ups and the evening roll-calls.

If the numbers on the early parade were insufficient, Abe would threaten to inspect the prisoners' huts. Once and for all he would throw out the malingerers (who, by the way, were dying at the rate of ten a day). Yet he carried out his threat only once, in the company of a silent and respectful medical student.

In the dysentery ward, he declared half the patients fit for work. The exempted half were the skeletonic cases lying naked, untended and alone. So few medical orderlies were available that "triage" had to be applied; only those who might possibly be saved were cared for.

After visiting the mephitic tropical ulcer hut, Abe kept silent. It was unnerving to discover a denuded shinbone, fingers pared down to sinews, a knee-joint half destroyed. The enfeebled immune system and the utter lack of drugs caused septicaemia to set in very fast. Maggots from the latrines were introduced into the gaping holes to eat away the putrid flesh; as we possessed no suture thread, red ants were made to close their mandibles on the edges of the wounds; and leaves were used as bandages.

All the malaria cases were ordered out, with the exception of those who, dying of the cerebral strain, were delirious and teetered on the edge of madness.

The men afflicted with beri-beri of the wet, or oedematous, type, were so dramatically swollen that nothing was said about pushing them out to work. The diphtheria patients were left alone, and no one went near the "jungle ward" where the odd cases of typhus, spinal meningitis and smallpox had been isolated.

His hospital tour over, Abe walked away with an expression I'd never seen before on his face: instead of flying off into a rage, he looked concerned.

"You understand, because you are a soldier," he explained once more to Colonel Hingston (this was his party piece), "that in war orders must be given until final victory. Sometimes, these orders are very hard, very painful. You must remember that the Emperor himself wants this railway to be built. As far as you are concerned, *shigata ga nai*, there's nothing you can do about it. Tomorrow, you find fifty more men."

Hingston and I refrained from looking at each other: we had expected closer to five hundred. Abe, clearly, had been very surprised.

Evening roll-call took an average of two and a half hours during which all movement in the camp was forbidden. The shortest time, according to my diary, was one hour; the longest, eight. In the dark, everyone had to be accounted for: the parties back from work; the sick, the dying and the dead; those who worked inside the camp; and those in isolation wards in the jungle. But how could we keep track of those who had simply walked out of the camp (there was no barbed wire or even defined boundaries) and disappeared in the jungle? Or drowned in the river? Or escaped? It was an impossible task ever to reconcile the figures. They had to be "cooked" but in such a way that they were acceptable to the Japanese. Whichever way they had been juggled, it had to be so cunningly done that our Sergeant Kanamoto, the *honcho*, would never lose face by pretending merely to believe them: the numbers had to carry conviction.

One evening in July, Colonel Banno's truck was reported bogged down in the mud, a mile from the camp. This was a common occurrence, and teams of fifty prisoners were assembled at all hours of the day or the night to rescue immobilised vehicles. By the time Banno arrived in Sonkurai, roll-call had been going on for four hours, and he announced that he was taking over the count.

Notebook in hand, accompanied by a couple of his officers and by an N.C.O. carrying a candle, old Banno started counting the prisoners one by one. In the working huts, this was easy as the men stood up in rows. It was in the hospital that the trouble started. The patients were made to number in the dark: some knew the Japanese digits, others not; some were confused and counted themselves twice, while others were comatose and in no state to understand what was required of them.

A corporal in my own division's Provost Company was lying at the edge of the platform. It was his turn to number off, but he remained silent. As an orderly gently shook him by the shoulder, his head fell back, the breath left his gaping mouth, and he died. Banno looked shaken.

Counting resumed. In the ulcer ward, it was impossible to make out if, lying by a pillar, there was a man or merely a bundle of rags. Banno climbed on the bamboo platform, candle in hand: crumpled under a piece of sackcloth, flesh rent with suppurating ulcers, he found a man. Like a fragment from a Gothic Inferno, two emaciated arms rose to the light in a wordless supplication.

Banno backed away. The hand holding the candle was trembling. "I thought he was dead," he whispered to me. Turning to an orderly, he said harshly, "You're not doing your duty. You can't allow a patient, one of your own comrades, to lie naked on the bamboo." And to me, "Let's hope he dies tonight."

The roll-call did not tally, and Banno, giving up, went off to sleep. At two a.m. the figures were made to work. Banno was woken up and told that everything, at last, was O.K.

Between morning line-up and evening roll-call, there was work – keeping the road open, laying embankments, building the bridge.

Trees were felled, stripped and dragged over long distances through the undergrowth. However hard men pulled, at times they could hardly move the log. Then a small, helmeted Japanese would start yelling and bring down his bamboo stick or wire whip on the men's backs; or kicking them in the shins. He might eventually call on the services of a mahout and his elephant. "One erephant samu eighty purisona," the Engineers had worked out. It was their favourite quote and joke.

Another group of men were detailed to build the road. Some men carried stones on stretchers from quarries to the road, others laid them down, and another team placed the logs over the stones.

At midday, food was taken out to the working parties, who were given an hour's break. A few fiends among the guards would select a small number of prisoners and take them into the jungle, for a special job, so they said. But there, away from the censure of their comrades, they indulged in sadistic conduct. Often one of our men ran back to the camp and reported the matter. I passed it on to our sergeant. At best, Banno would hear of it a week later, but nothing could ever be done: the culprit was an Engineer.

Long after dark, the parties came back. In theory they never saw the camp in daylight; in practice everyone was down, because of malaria, one day in five. Towards mid-June work on the road slackened, and the erection of the railway bridge, well behind schedule, began. Day and night shifts were organised, and although the work was more interesting than road repair, it was extremely hard because of the heavy logs that had to be hewn and shifted into position.

At that time it was a simple timber road bridge, 120 feet long and 20 feet wide. It rose only about six feet above the water. When the rain swelled the river, in the first week of July, it looked as if the current would sweep away everything. Commanded by Abe, all the Japanese Engineers stood on the bridge, fishing out logs and debris that accumulated against the pilings.

In order to bring the top of the bridge level with the future railway embankment, it was necessary to raise it from where it stood, level with the road, to a height of about 30 feet. Apart from tools, the only material brought by truck for the construction of such an important work were forged steel "dogs" which joined one log to another. The work was dangerous, especially at night when the illumination was provided by acetylene lamps, and men often fell into the water. Two or three broke their limbs, but the Japs fared as badly. On more than one occasion, a prisoner was struck by an Engineer and thrown into the river.

The Engineers squeezed the work-force harder. Even those whose feet had rotted away, who were unable to make their way unaided, reported at the morning line-up, carried and deposited on the ground. They went to work, propelling themselves through the mud, slithering on their backsides, and using a bamboo stick to pole themselves forward. They were known as "the gondoliers".

The trunks of large teak trees were being sunk into the river bed, and the gondoliers were harnessed to the pile-driver, a simple three-legged derrick guyed down on four sides. For twelve hours they pulled and released a rope lashed to the monkey, a cast-iron weight weighing 600 pounds.

During that flap, when everyone, prisoners and Engineers, was trying to save the bridge, once again I escorted an inspecting Japanese officer to the river. He was, he told me, a student of *Mein Kampf,* and an admirer of Adolf Hitler. Not many Japanese were concerned with the Jews, but he had made them his special study. "In fact," he went on to say, "I can recognise a Jew a hundred metres away."

We reached the bridge as the whistle blew to announce the noon break. Fifty prisoners, most of them naked, climbed out of the river. The visiting major looked at them in amazement: "I didn't know you had so many Jews in the British Army," he said as the prisoners, a good number of them circumcised, went by him to pick up their "jap-happies".

Hoping that one day he would cover himself in ridicule, I did nothing to correct his illusions.

If they weren't happy with the morning body count, the Engineers had another way of making life a little more miserable: they withheld the tools needed for camp duties. We had three or four shovels that we'd carried all the way from Banpong, but we needed many more, along with crosscut saws, axes and hoes.

"If you couldn't provide the men we asked for, who's left to use these tools? Or have you been lying to us?" asked the Engineers.

We appealed to Kanamoto, the *honcho.* But he knew they would not give him a hearing, and he wasn't ready to lose face before us. So we broke bamboo with our bare hands, the latrines overflowed, the corpses piled up as they couldn't be cremated, and the huts went without fires.

After a few days, the Engineers would give in and allow us a few tools. They'd had their fun. And when our chief medical officer reminded them that unless the corpses were disposed of the plague would carry them off as fast as it would kill us, they listened.

They had, however, a more immediate concern: food wasn't reaching us any more.

At first, in addition to the watery breakfast pap, twice a day we had been getting a pint of cooked rice. Hiding in it, like nuggets, we discovered a few beans, or strands of meat. A herd of yaks (as we refered to bullocks) had been driven into the camp before our arrival, and we slaughtered the animals who looked as if they were about to die.

But by the end of June, even bullock carts had to stop short of Sonkurai, and for a few days a different attempt was made to bring supplies. The Japanese released one elephant from the working pool. This was insufficient; the average adult male can carry no more than three hundred pounds, including its mahout, who claimed that the mud was too deep for his great beast, and the rewards too thin for him. He downed tools, as it were.

The elephant was replaced by prisoners harnessed to carts. The idea was abandoned after the first trip, and from then on every other day a party of fifty men was sent on foot to Changaraya, No. 5 Camp, immediately below the Three Pagodas Pass where supplies came down from Burma. They brought back rice, and like our captors we regarded the stuff as sacred: every grain embodied the essence of life. We watched the rice party returning in the twilight, looking like the mud-men of New Guinea. In their packs, they carried food for twelve hundred. These were lean days.

We hunted snakes, collected bamboo shoots and grubs, and tried to trap small animals like rats and monkeys, but in vain: feeding off the jungle is a full time job. A rubber planter who knew the Sakais, the pygmies of the Malay forest, described how a family started gathering its food at first light in order to secure their evening meal.

And like the Sakais we craved salt. Unlike them, however, we had nothing to deposit at the foot of trees and expect, the following day, to find salt brought by traders in exchange for jungle products. I suffered from excruciating itching, waking up at night in a frenzy of scratching. So did my neighbour, who had practised law in Kuala Lumpur. We reported sick. "Salt deficiency," said the M.O. "Nothing to be done about it."

I thought otherwise. I cut a six inch length of thin bamboo, and by punching out the inner woody membranes, I ended up with a smooth tube. One end was slashed to a sharp point.

With the instrument in my pocket, I went to the Japanese cookhouse and requested the cook to help me with a point of grammar. He was pleased to be thought a scholar.

From the start of the lesson, I stood leaning against bags of salt that lined a whole wall of the cookhouse. With my hand in my pocket, I jammed the sharp end of the tube into one of the bags. The salt trickled down through the tube, and the lesson was made to drag out until my pocket was filled. Thanking the cook for his trouble, triumphantly I returned to our part of the camp.

My legal friend and I took handfuls of the stuff and jammed it into our mouths. Night came, and along with it, the terrible and unabated itch. The M.O. confirmed that the action wasn't instantaneous. Three days later, however, there was no improvement.

I mentioned our lack of success to a sergeant-major whose diagnosis was different.

"If I may say so," he told me, "because you and your friend are gentlemen you probably haven't bothered to look for lice. But I would if I were you."

We did, and to our horror we found that our shorts had become a suitable, if somewhat overcrowded, habitat for the vermin. Of course, they were "bamboo lice": everyone else harboured plain body lice.

Obsession with food overwhelmed all emotions, and snuffed out common humanity. Crime, prevalent in Banpong, was rife in Sonkurai. Money being almost non-existent, barter became the *modus operandi*. And barter required an ever-flowing supply of goods. The traffic rested on three legs; the prisoners who provided the goods, the coolies who acted as go-betweens, and the traders, Thai or Burmese, who supplied food and tobacco.

Large reinforcements of coolies arrived as the Engineers realised that F Force was spent and useless. These Tamils, Thais, Burmese and Chinese suffered far more than we did. Their rations were suppposedly equal to ours, but they had to buy them back from the Japanese who openly looted them. They had no doctors, and the only medical care they ever received was one prophylactic quinine tablet daily. The test applied by the Engineers when a coolie reported sick was to administer a sound thrashing: if the man died, well, he would have died anyway, it was no loss; and if he went to work, no better proof was needed that he had been malingering all along.

For me, ungifted for commerce, it was a constant wonder that in the thick of the Thai jungle trade could flourish. It wasn't exclusively fuelled by crime, although if you lacked anything to sell, and if you couldn't supply a service, theft was the way out. Rice – which we craved above all – was generally stolen for self-consumption. But if a yak could be led astray, it would be discreetly slaughtered with picks and shovels (this could only be done outside the camp, by one of the working parties), and part of the meat sold. And if the animal died of disease and was buried, it was sure to be exhumed overnight, and sold, regardless of health risks.

The Japanese had forbidden any cooking in the huts in the hope of putting a stop to the black market, but it served no purpose. Their rules were made to be broken. They found proof of our villainy when they observed that the limited number of blankets which, after much discussion and pleading on our part, they had released to us, had disappeared: along with perfectly serviceable British Army clothing, the blankets turned up during a search of the coolie lines. At night we shivered, and during the day we walked about practically naked. Food, however, was the paramount need.

We owned little, so that the disappearance of a single object could lead to death. The theft of a mess-tin, for instance, meant waiting for someone to finish his rice, and then borrowing his. But by that time there might be nothing left at the bottom of the *kwali*. If most people were conscious of the consequences of stealing from an individual, fewer hesitated when the opportunity arose to loot commonly owned stores. The pressure to survive blunted the finer points of ethics.

Crime took many shapes. Certain senior N.C.O.s kept men off working parties in exchange for bribes: a sick man would then have to take the place of a fitter and wealthier companion. A successful black-marketeer might defer his profits to the post-war period: he'd approach a desperately sick man and ask him what he thought he needed to save himself. "An egg a day for ten days, and I know I'll make it," wasn't an unusual answer. "Sign a chit then. You'll owe me £500 payable when we're liberated," the dealer would say. It was a time when a skilled workman was making five pounds a week.

Some officers shammed illness in order to avoid working parties. Yet when volunteers were requested to go to Nikki and back in one day and collect canteen supplies, many were instantly available.

Men joined forces for mutual support and in order to hunt food more efficiently. Within the groups themselves, the two-man unit was the most cohesive and offered the greatest hope of survival. Not surprisingly, the usual factor that led to bonding was a common social background. And yet the integration of an individual in a supportive group was not by itself sufficient to ensure survival. There needed to be a strong personal determination to overcome the suffering of the body, the withdrawal of the most elementary satisfactions, and the ever more evanescent hope of coming out of it alive.

I'm thinking of L., a charming and cultivated friend. He was physically strong – he rowed for his Oxford college – and mentally gifted; his mind was incisive and his speech elegant. It was equally evident that he was ill-equipped to deal with what the French call *les détails matériels de la vie*. Because of his exceptional qualities he always found friends to take care of him, and ensure his well-being. He was a "life-enhancer". We didn't want to lose him.

L. started the march comfortably. In the early stages, however, when the columns still moved in semi-populated areas, a terrible thing happened to him: he'd placed the whole of his kit on a bullock cart from which it was stolen, except for the haversack he was carrying. Inevitably this meant great hardship, although, all along the way he received help from a friend who shared his blanket and mess-tin. When he arrived in Sonkurai, although not ill, he was weak. And much of his *amour-propre* had gone; he did not bother to wash or shave. We managed to keep him off road and bridge, and got him a cushy job right in camp – just boiling water all day. Whatever the reasons he wasn't able to hold the job, and he was sent out to work for Abe and his murderous Engineers. L.'s health and morale then declined fast. Once more, with the proper approach to the N.C.O. responsible for detailing the working parties (an approach usely accompanied by a twist of Sikh's Beard or the remants of a Marmite jar), we kept him in camp for a few days. Once again, the few remnants of his kit were stolen. All he owned in this world were a grubby singlet, a shirt in shreds and a few rags around his middle. He was sick of life and despairing. He hadn't washed for two months, and however much we talked to him, nothing and no one managed to change his attitude.

He declined and was moved to a hospital hut. The downward slide continued. His friends brought him such extreme rarities as tinned milk, fish and soap. But he was so little interested in the business of living that he gave them away. He died very quietly of disgust and hopelessness two and a half months after his arrival in Sonkurai.

EIGHT

One evening, towards the end of June, Robinson came to see me. He was a lieutenant in the Royal Army Service Corps, and we had struck up a friendship; how and where I have forgotten. He hoisted himself up on the platform, and I made room for him to sit on my folded blanket.

The fires burning in the aisle were down to embers, and in the vast hut darkness lapped at us like a foetid tide. But my lamp – a twist of cotton propped up in a tin of palm oil – was burning with a deep yellow flame. The tiny circle of light seemed a rock barely emerging above the surface of the sea, a refuge for shipwrecked sailors.

I was writing up my diary on scraps of paper which I'd stolen from the Japanese office. That day Louis, the astute Frenchman in my unit who had made a killing on currency during the journey to Banpong, had given me a small Burma cheroot, and I carefully halved it. I still owned my Army Issue knife with its spike designed to extract small stones from horses' hooves. The steel was excellent and the blade had been honed so finely that I used it as a cut-throat razor. Bending our heads down to the level of the lamp, we lit up.

"Listen carefully," said Robinson. He was speaking in low tones, almost whispering, his words blurred by the staccato of the rain hitting the atap roof. "I've got important news." Since our first days in Changi, Robinson had been determined to get away. Now an escape party, he revealed, had been formed, and he asked me if I would be part of it.

This wasn't of course the first time the question had come up. But, whenever I thought of it, I found it difficult to sort out its different options. King's Rules & Regulations, the British soldier's legal code, specified that it was the British soldier's legal duty to escape. However, failure to toe the K.R.R. line never engendered acute feelings of guilt. But what if the opportunity presented itself? My uppermost consideration was my role as interpreter. Were I to disappear, at least for a while the disorganisation and the misery of life in Sonkurai were sure to get worse. Yet, viewed objectively, our chances of staying alive much longer were thin. Should I not try and save myself? *Primum vivere.*

Two groups had already escaped from Sonkurai, earlier on in June, a few days after their arrival. Cholera had just broken out, and the survival of the 1,600 prisoners was questionable. Low on food, ill-prepared and ill-equipped but urged on by despair, a dozen men from the Manchester Regiment were the first to leave. They were reported to the Japanese; had they been recaptured, or had their absence been noticed, Lieutenant Colonel Pope, the camp's senior officer, would have had to bear the consequences, most likely death, for aiding and abetting them. The second escape party was composed of eight Eurasians from one of the regiments recruited in Malaya: some spoke Thai, others Burmese; they had money, jewels, drugs and firearms. Their intention was to make their way to the Indian border by bullock cart, travelling openly as merchants. A measure of the chaos that prevailed at the time in Sonkurai is that neither the guards nor the Engineers took the slightest action. They dismissed the news, finding it more convenient to believe that the escapes hadn't happened at all.

(I never found out whether they made it or not. As for the Manchesters, they hid in a cave close to a Thai village until the end of '43, when one of them ran off with what little money they still possessed. The villagers had no more use for them and promptly turned them over to the Japanese; the same fate overtook the thief when his money ran out.)

Louis was working in the Engineers' tool store. He was as successful in Sonkurai as everywhere else, and as generous. I found myself in the curious position, however, of being his *directeur de conscience.* Louis might come up with a borderline or downright unacceptable idea for bettering his material status, and I'd have to say to him, "If you do this, I'll never speak to you again." In exchange for friendship and advice, I'd receive, like any good curate, a contribution to my welfare.

A week or two before Robinson's proposal, Louis had been approached by a Burmese. He was the interpreter and go-between with the Japanese, and he had offered help in planning an escape. Simply talking it over with him was a risky business; the Burmese could well have been setting up a trap. Louis's hunch, however, was that the fellow could be trusted. The plan was to send him to the coast where he would buy and provision a fishing boat; then come back to Sonkurai with an elephant that would carry Louis and myself through the jungle. But nothing came of it: on the day he was due to leave, the Burmese got cold feet and dropped the idea.

I asked Robinson for details of the escape plan.

So far ten men had been "signed up". Heading the party was Lieutenant Colonel Wilkinson, Royal Engineers, a yachtsman; the other seaman was James Bradley, a lieutenant; Robinson himself was to be navigator; Sonkurai's quartermaster, Lieutenant Anker, would supply food; Lieutenant Jones of the Malay Regiment spoke Burmese and was familiar with travel in the jungle; and Private Brown of the Straits Settlements Volunteer Force had expert knowledge of the country to be crossed. Three more lieutenants and an Indian cook from the Burmese coolie camp completed the list. The cook was a fisherman, a native of Chittagong on the Bay of Bengal, who wanted to go home. Once on the Burma coast, the British would go into hiding while he would buy a boat. All would then set sail westward.

As the crow flies, less than fifty miles separated Sonkurai and the coast. Crossing the jungle I judged to be beyond our physical ability. On the ground, following game trails or hacking through the undergrowth, the fifty miles were likely to be tripled. They could never be covered in the three weeks the ten men had allotted themselves. No, I wouldn't join Wilkinson's escape party. Robinson asked me not to mention the matter to anyone. I borrowed his map of the region, printed on silk, made a copy of it, and never gave any further thought to the project.

On July 11, at 8 a.m. Major Price, who was adjutant at the time, came to see me to say that Major Wilkinson, seven officers and one other rank had escaped. What should we do in regard to the Japanese? At first, no one among us had missed the escape party; it was simply thought they had gone off on fatigues, but at breakfast the truth became clear.

Colonel Hingston, who slept next to Wilkinson, now understood what had happened a couple of hours earlier. He had gone to the latrine where he had found Wilkinson. They went back together to their hut, but later Hingston heard some activity next to him and asked his neighbour if he was all right. Wilkinson just answered that he couldn't sleep.

We reported the escape to our Japanese sergeant, who at the time was sick with malaria. He was lying on the floor of his hut, under his mosquito net, and when I spoke to him, "*Honcho dono*, there's something I must tell you", he didn't react at all; he turned over and grunted. I did away with the preamble and came to the point. "*Honcho dono*, ten men have escaped!" The sergeant was on his feet in a spring-like motion. He went pale and let out a stupendous roar, "*Tenko! Hayaku shite!*" – roll-call! Hurry! A second roar was addressed to his men; they too were to parade and load five rounds in their rifles. After roll-call, the guards went off looking for the escapees.

At ten a.m., Lieutenant Fukuda came up from Shimo Sonkurai in order to interrogate all those officers who had slept next to the escaped men. I believed it was essential that they should not tell the truth – that they knew nothing – and that they should invent their own stories. Otherwise the Japanese would certainly think they were lying. Unfortunately there was no time to warn them, and Fukuda, in a threatening mood, told them to go back and reconsider their declarations.

Soon after, and only a few minutes before Colonel Banno himself arrived, Hingston found under his pillow a letter from Wilkinson. He showed it to me, and asked whether Banno should see it. My main concern was that Hingston not be accused of aiding the escape, so I said yes. I was sure the letter would whitewash him. Of course it was incredible, on the face of things, that neither Hingston nor anyone else should know of the escape plan. Apart from myself it is likely that the only other man in the know was a medical officer who supplied the medicines, shown as Major X in my diary. I didn't write down the initial of his name in case my diary was ever discovered, and now I can't remember who it was). The letter ran as follows:

Dear Uncle, this is to tell you the news of our 'desertion'. We had decided to try and escape long ago, and to save you the trouble of finding out the personnel of the party, here are their names [the party's roster followed]. I am sorry to put you on the spot but our minds have been made up. We are well equipped and with the help of God, and if our legs carry us, we hope to reach the outside world and let them know of your plight. Sorry to cause you all this trouble. [Signed] Wilky.

P.S. Try and delay the news of our departure for 24 hours.

Along with Banno came Koryasu, the gruff Japanese interpreter, so that I was a mere witness of the meeting between the two colonels. Banno declared the letter was a forgery and quickly came to the point.

"Colonel Hingston," he said, "I am sorry, but I shall have to shoot you."

"Sir! I protest most strongly!" replied Hingston.

After a half-hour discussion, Banno agreed to suspend his decision if a complete admission of guilt was forthcoming. In the meantime all the officers, with the exception of those accompanying working parties, would be deprived of food. Sentries were posted at each end of their huts. (At night we managed to smuggle food through, and the order was rescinded after forty-eight hours.) Although pure inventions, detailed accounts of suspicious movements observed several days before the escape were compiled and handed over. Banno appeared satisfied.

The Koreans were extremely upset. Those on guard duty thought they would be decapitated; all realised that they had been helping the escapees by selling them tinned food and changing, at a nice profit, Thai money for Burmese. They were reinforced by an officer and twenty men, all Japanese. The warning given was simple: if anyone escaped, everybody would be shot. Three weeks later, we heard that four survivors had been picked up near the coast.

Robinson wasn't among the four officers who were brought back to Sonkurai where they were going to be shot *pour encourager les autres*. He was the second to die (of toxaemia from ulcerated hands), after Wilkinson, the biggest man in the party. We tried to give the four survivors as much food and comfort as we could.

They were placed in a small bamboo hut near the river where they had just enough room to lie down. Once a day one of our officers brought them food, and news was exchanged until the Koreans put a stop to it.

Colonel Banno, to quote my diary, "showed them great kindness".

They had left with the belief that beyond the hills visible on the other side of the river the country would be flatter. The information was terribly wrong; they had to traverse steep hills, hacking their way through bamboo. In order to hide the smoke of their fires they slept in valleys. The monsoon never let up. Daily they covered about ten miles on the ground, but the effective distance westward was two and never more than three miles. Two weeks after their departure, they were still only halfway to their goal, without food, physically spent, wracked with fever, and poisoned by tropical ulcers. They ate leaves and bamboo shoots. In the morning they buried the dead.

The four survivors reached a swamp from which they could see Allied aircraft dropping bombs on Ye, a small town on the Burma coast. The swamp led to a swift river. They built a raft which overturned in rapids, losing all their belongings as well as their money. They swam to the shore where local Burmese helped them out of the water and carried them (they were incapable of walking) to the hut of the village chief, who fed them. The following day, he gave them a guide to lead them to the coast. They knew they were going to be denounced, but in their condition there was no alternative. They waited for their fate in the house they had been taken to. In the morning, two armed Japanese arrested them. They were brought to the Moulmein jail before being escorted back to Sonkurai.

Colonel Banno accused the officers in the escape party of abandoning their men.

"No, Colonel Banno," answered Colonel Harris, senior officer of F Force, who had also arrived in Sonkurai, "they did it to let the world know how the Japanese treat their prisoners on the Thai Railway. We were told to trust the Imperial Japanese Army. When we left Singapore with our sick men, we were assured no harm would come to us. Three months later, out of the seven thousand who trusted the I.J.A. seventeen hundred are dead."

Colonel Banno started to weep.

The four survivors were spared. Probably, Harris's letter to Banno, in which he presented himself as the British Government's representative turned the trick:

> Sir, I have the honour to inform you that yesterday I was told by Lieut. Yamada that some British officers had been arrested for escape, that they would probably be condemned to death, and that I must hold myself in readiness to witness the execution.
>
> If this is so, as senior British officer and therefore the Representative of the British Government on the spot, I wish to make a formal appeal to the Imperial Japanese Government (on behalf of the British Government) not to enact the death penalty.

In Sonkurai almost all the commissioned officers disapproved of the escape: they were incensed at the nine men's "desertion", the word used by Wilkinson in his letter. Their argument was that it wasn't known at the time whether collective reprisals would be taken or not; and that every fit man was desperately needed to lighten the suffering of the sick. Colonel Dillon's opinion being that "men without their officers are dead men," he too must have disapproved of the scheme.

After the second escape party – that of the Eurasians – it had been publicly announced that permission for escapes would not be given. And Jones, the expert on the country to be traversed, had been lied to: he was ill at the time the Wilkinson party was set afoot, and he had no wish to be part of it. Yet, as his knowledge was needed, he had been told that Hingston had given his approval to the scheme. Jones was one of those who died in the jungle.

The O.R.s, however, had a diametrically opposite attitude. They all said, "Good luck to them."

It must have been the time when the Allied air forces started their raids in the region, such as the attack on Ye. One afternoon, for the first time, we saw a fleet of four-engine American bombers (they were Liberators, we learned later) travelling west.

We stood literally transfixed with joy. We were convinced that no one in the outside world had ever heard of the Siam-Burma railway. Nor had we ever seen such monsters with four engines, two on each wing. Japanese Zero fighters rose to intercept. A Japanese pilot deliberately directed his aircraft against one of the huge friendly machines. Both went down blazing.

The newly arrived Japanese officer addressed us after roll-call. A wooden box was brought so that he could stand over us. He spoke some English, and I wasn't required to translate the speech.

"Engurish purisona," he bellowed, "I see how you look at American bombers. I see you are very happy. But happinesss is not correct. American poruduction so bad, so many mistakes, much too many engines for number of bomber planes. So necessary attach four engines to each plane. Dismiss!"

Later that day, sensing that his officer's words had perhaps not achieved the desired effect, a corporal confided to me another piece of news: the population of London was rioting – there was no more rice in the warehouses.

We had heard extraordinary but also disturbing news. The sick who weren't expected to recover within two months were going to be shipped to a new hospital camp in Burma. It could only be a death camp.

On the other hand, the Japanese described it as a near paradise, a land of milk-and-honey. But we hadn't forgotten the promise of the Cameron Highlands, and no one believed the new fabulations.

A Korean guard arrived in Sonkurai with a letter from Colonel Harris. In it were outlined the organisation of a hospital for twelve hundred men; the specifications for the personnel, medical and otherwise, that would staff it; and the composition of the advance party. Hutch was appointed commanding officer; Major Hunt, an Australian, chief medical officer; and myself interpreter.

Without any warning, one morning during the first week of August, the nucleus of the advance party arrived in Sonkurai from Nikki. We were told to be ready to depart in half an hour, enough to pack our few belongings, and no time at all to take leave of our friends. We plodded off to Changaraya, only eight kilometres away, where we spent the night (and ate far better than at Sonkurai; for reasons no one could make out Sonkurai was the nadir of all camps). We were joined by the men of the other advance parties, so that in all we numbered seventy, two-thirds of which were medical personnel, British and Australian. The first stage of the journey was by lorry.

Around noon we crossed the Three Pagodas Pass. In a life starved of romance, we had imagined this landmark to be a crag in the rock, high in the hills, surmounted by three white shining pagodas. The reality was distinctly other: the road was actually flatter and dustier than usual, and on the left stood three moth-eaten pagodas with a papier-mâché look. A thick tree trunk planed down on one side announced in Japanese the name of the pass.

(1979)

The truck stops for business at a village, a cluster of a dozen houses scattered around a general store. Behind the store, entwined in lianas, and two-thirds hidden under tropical growth, I spot an old Marmon lorry picked clean of everything that was removable.

Cases of Fanta are unloaded, and a man with grey hair boards the rear of the truck. The Princeton girl makes signs that we're about to leave, and calls me to come back.

The new passenger, having asked who I am, tells Aung Song that he served here as a police officer during the war. "Every day," he says, "boom boom at two o'clock in the afternoon: American and English planes." It must have been towards the end of the war as in 1943 there were no Thai officials anywhere in the region; this is confirmed when the ex-policeman adds that the men who worked at the time on the railway were Malays, Burmese and Indians, not P.O.W.s.

The three pagodas on our left are the only sign that the border has been crossed. Newly whitewashed, they stand twenty feet high on crumbling brick foundations at the edge of the forest: *Phra Chedi*, the three pagodas that were erected in the eighteenth century by the kings of Burma and of Siam. One stood on Burmese soil, the other on Thai; and at the foot of the middle one they signed a covenant signifying that they would no longer war against each other. These days the triple stupas serves a dual purpose: commercial when their image appears in advertisements and on packaged goods; and ritual to invoke good luck (with a dash of regional loyalty) when painted on the side-panels of trucks and Land Rovers.

Spanning their elegant spires a wire has been stretched: from it hang, purely for their decorative effect, three burnt-out electric lightbulbs.

Monks in yellow and orange robes wave at us from the entrance of their diminutive monastery. A new and very large one is being built on the opposite side of the road.

A mile down from the Pass we stop at the village. Like the other settlements built during the past decade in the Kwai basin it spreads out on both sides of the road. It's also journey's end for motor vehicles: from here on, only a track leads into Burma.

The thatched houses with their verandahs and flowering bushes nestle in bowers of lacy bamboo groves; the fronds of large trees arch over the roofs; and through the smoke of charcoal fires the sun's slanting rays throw splotches of blue light.

The road serves as village square, agora and recreation park. It's here that convoys of carts laden with contraband assemble before pursuing their journey to Burma. Uniformed Mon despatch-riders gallop on their ponies, brandishing their automatic rifles. Outside the three general stores which double up as inns, people meet to shop and gossip, and bare-bottomed children play soldiers on the doorsteps of houses. A bullock-cart delivers a sack of rice to be husked and polished at the door of the mill, humming and murmuring all day long. Coveys of small pink pigs root in the ditches, and humpbacked oxen drift about, lazily nibbling away at clumps of grass. Sitting in deep puddles, water-buffalos ruminate. I thought: this place is beautiful, this place pleases me. I'm reminded of the Chinese proverb, "The wise man never leaves his village."

The three hundred villagers, all Mons, live in some fifty houses, and cultivate hill-rice, a small-grain strain which doesn't have to grow with its feet in water, in patches of cleared jungle. Smuggling, however, is their mainstay. Socialist Burma, attempting to be self-sufficient, bans the importation of all non-essential goods. Consequently the black economy is not only thriving but openly tolerated by the authorities; either as supplier or consumer, everyone is involved. From large machine parts to sewing needles, the bullock-carts bring into the country an unending variety of industrial and especially consumer goods. The demand for *aji-no-moto*, a Japanese condiment made from fish-bones and monosodium glutamate is so great that a factory has been set up in Thailand strictly to supply the smugglers. The

Three Pagoda Pass is their point of entry, and from Burma they bring out cattle, rubies, gold and silver, and jade.

The bullock-cart convoys operate every day. During the monsoon season, when they would get mired in the mud, they're replaced by elephant carts. But the elephants are banned from the track: their great weight and the heavy carts would destroy it. They have to make their own trails through the forest.

At a checkpoint beyond the village, Mon and Karen soldiers levy a toll on traffic in both directions. The Karens are neighbours and the prime fighters in the unending struggle for independence from Rangoon.

For all the agrestic aspects of Phra Chedi, it's the presence of the M.N.L.A., the Mon National Liberation Army, that gives its nervous and almost dynamic tone. Our arrival must have been known in advance, for no sooner do we jump off the truck than a boy in uniform instructs us where to report.

Aung Song speaks to the driver, who takes us to a substantial two-storey teak house and carries our gear to the top of the stairs.

A captain and two lieutenants greet us. This is an M.N.L.A. depot; rows of weapons, mostly of American and German manufacture, are stacked in corners and along walls. Aung Song installs my bedroll under the Buddha altar. A batman enters and serves us tea from a Chinese thermos flask enlivened with decals of chubby little girls; I turn down an offer of betel which an old man is neatly slicing up with a special device like a giant cigar-cutter.

I'm asked the purpose of my journey: it's to find out, I answer, whether it will be possible to go up to the bridge I believe is still standing, some thirty or forty kilometres from here. Someone else, I'm informed, will give me an answer.

In another house I'm introduced to a sickly-looking man seated in a deckchair. He's the vice-chairman of the Mon State Party. "Yes," he says, "permission has been received. You may go to the bridge at Apparon. This captain will head your escort tomorrow." I shake hands with the captain, a young man in green combat fatigues.

A wonderful meal has been prepared: curry of wild deer; roast boar; fish and vegetables. No beer as we're still in the Reverend Ottama's parish.

At the end of the meal the village headman comes to announce that dances are planned in my honour tonight. "You are an original inhabitant of Phra Chedi," he says. "You were here long before any of us." They are very pleased that I should have come to visit the village; it's not the first time they have received a Westerner, but no ex-P.O.W. has ever bothered to come up this far.

Three hours before the start of the dances I move from house to house and watch the actors making up by the light of candles and oil lamps. In their dark huts, these men and women I've seen in the fields barefoot and in tatters, sit on a mat, small mirrors propped up against the bamboo wall, and transmute themselves into ancient courtiers. Gold and silver dust, white pomades, lipsticks, black eye makeup, rouge, unguents of green, mauve and yellow hues, and coloured talcums are taken out of their tiny wood and metal boxes. Slowly, almost languorously, they are applied with finger and paintbrush on forehead, eyebrows, eyelids, cheeks and mouths.

A permanent stage lit by an acetylene lamp has been set up in a jungle clearing, a hundred feet off the road. Around the pool of light, the jungle is black and impenetrable. First to arrive are the food and betel-nut vendors; by nine o'clock, when the representation starts, the children have been installed up front, and the Mon garrison, fully armed, stands at the back. The whole village is present, seated on the ground. The head drummer in his pit, a barrel of wood and woven reed, sounds the overture on his eighteen drums. Cymbals, bells, kettledrums and thin reeds pick up the cue, a mélange of Balinese gamelan instructed in the distant past by Chinese court music.

Of the forty performers, the youngest are two very small four-year-old girls, and the oldest a lean and graceful man in his seventies. A first round of improvisations in song, dance and story telling announces that we're to be transported back to the eighteenth century, to the life at the court of the Mon King, in his capital of Pegu.

One by one the performers advance to the proscenium, take three steps and freeze in convoluted stances. Applause and shouts of admiration greet the pink and plum silks, the peacock blue calicos, the feathered headdresses, the glitter and the pearls.

Drawing from each one their own excellence, the head dancer leads a turn with all forty performers.

And now unfold the stories of war-riddled kings, immensely wise monkey-priests and immensely compassionate elephants, danced by lithe bodies moving sinuously before a naive backdrop of palaces and pagodas.

Undulating hands, polychrome faces, bird-like turns of heads, and provocative eyes; Asiatic sensualities and archaic memories embodied in these Mon peasants who, wanting to honour me, have recalled in a jungle clearing the past glory of their King and his people.

Humbly, I thank the performers, the villagers and the village chief. The dances lasted three and a half hours.

(1943)

The Three Pagodas Pass was the watershed. The Australian and Dutch prisoners we met on the Burma side we pronounced fit: they weren't cadaver thin, they didn't have empty eyes.

There was hope then: hope, more precisely, that at Tambaya, the new hospital camp, we wouldn't be starving. But we also knew that the treatment of prisoners was capricious, and it was never possible to understand why one group fared well, and another abominably. At Kyandaw, the next stage, we found a dispirited squad of British M.O.s. They had been taken out of Changi six months before and led to believe they would run the medical services in coolie camps. The reality turned out differently: while some served as cooks and batmen to a Japanese anti-malarial platoon, others were put to unloading barges and felling trees. All were harshly treated.

We shared a hut with Burmese coolies. Their inexhaustible vitality and their rowdiness deprived us of sleep. They had devised a radical way of dealing with the desperately ill: anyone unable to feed himself unaided was simply shoved beneath the sleeping platform. When the smell of decomposition became too high, the body was taken out.

We explained to the Japanese that if our own sick on their way to Tambaya were to be housed with the Burmese they were sure to pick up additional diseases. We asked for shovels to clean out the excrement-covered floors. "Use your hands," we were told, and summarily dismissed. Our patients would be dead within a couple of months anyway, so why all the fuss?

We left Kyondaw the following evening and marched all night.

The rain which had held off all day now came down as if to make up for its long absence.

A streaky yellow dawn stained the sky as we reached the south bank of a river as wide as the Kwai. We crossed it on rafts. Its name, we learned, was the Apalon.

(1979)

The captain in charge of our small escort (a sergeant and three privates) assumes a military taciturnity. Eventually, through Aung Song, I get him to admit that from the Three Pagodas to our goal, the Apalon bridge, the distance is twenty-five kilometres.

We leave the road with its bullock-carts and foot-slogging smugglers, and enter the jungle.

It's early afternoon when we stumble across the old railway track, cutting straight through the undergrowth like a voracious caterpillar. Walking on these indestructible sleepers, eighteen inches apart, produces a false cadence: to step on each one engenders a mincing gait; and to skip one is to elongate one's stride unnaturally. The sensation is not new, and (a kinetic madeleine, this time) I recall the final stage to Tambaya along the newly completed track. I remember too the calculation someone had made (whether wildy approximate or not, it had the ring of good advertising copy), that for every sleeper a man had died.

In single file, we branch off into an overgrown trail, hardly discernible. The lead man slashes the undergrowth with his *parang*, and while we wait for the way to open Aung Song hums the names of the trees around us: teak, Malabar ironwood, yang, Burma padauk. Parasols of ferns hang over the trail; swinging lianas descend from the canopy; and aerial nets of creepers vault over our heads.

Brutally, the penumbra is flooded by the glare of the sky, and ghost-like, forlorn, desolate, a steel bridge soars above the river. A concrete pier supports the two spans. Incomprehensibly, the bridge appears to have been freshly painted a dirty shade of red, like coagulated blood. From up close, it is revealed to be nothing but deep rust, the effect highly chromatic in contrast with its complementary colour, the pervasive greenness of the jungle.

Later too, crossing over to the other bank, I understand why the structure appears intact, untouched by bombing: of the span linking the bridge to the western embankment nothing remains but blocks of concrete cocooned in mosses and creepers.

I strip and swim away from the bank. In midstream I let the slow current take me down, shouting to the Mons to come and join me. They're walking up and down the apron, scanning the banks; they wave but otherwise take no notice. A Burmese army patrol, they tell me later, is said to be in the vicinity.

(1943)

Two hours after crossing the Apalon on rafts, from the stillness of the forest we found ourselves suddenly transported (as it appeared to us) to a full-blown war zone. Reinforcements of men and transport, of field-guns and supplies of every kind had been assembled in a vast clearing. Not allowed to rest or linger in Mezali, as the place was named, we were ordered to climb into a truck.

We soon longed to be on foot again, fighting mud, rain and exhaustion. We pitched and rolled as the wheels foundered in deep ruts and joltingly climbed out. The fumes from the leaky exhaust seeped into our tarpaulin-covered truck, and we hung out in turns to vomit. This would be a sure way, we said, of reducing the number of patients bound for Tambaya.

By noon we reached Ronshii, the line's southernmost operational point. We found shelter in a dilapidated hut, and my diary, never failing to report any improvement in our diet, mentions that we bought *shindegar,* sugar made from unrefined palm oil, and cheroots. The journey had aggravated our symptoms. My dysentery had become so acute that I was given M&B sulphanomides. It was the enormous privilege of those who were considered "key personnel" to be treated with medicines from our tiny and ever dwindling supply; the decision was up to the senior M.O. with the approval of the British commanding officer.

Six miles only separated us from Tambaya. We walked them, stepping from one railway sleeper to another. On schedule, the rain accompanied us all the way.

Tambaya looked inhospitable on that bleak day. The camp straddled the railway line, nine dilapidated huts on the east side, three on the west. Before the war these huts had been part of a British coolie camp, and recently they had been occupied by the prisoners of A Force. Gangs of Burmese were at work, thatching and rebuilding walls. Only the Japanese sleeping quarters were completed, and we moved in with them.

The layout of the huts followed the usual pattern except for their narrowness; along their whole length only one, and not two bamboo platforms stood off the ground at a height varying from five to fifteen feet, depending on the slope of the terrain. In spite of the slope, the ground was waterlogged.

The following morning we set about designing a drainage system, putting up the cookhouse, digging latrines and building an incinerator. There were only seventy of us, unfit by any standard. To the pressure of completing the work before the patients' arrival, was added the strain, as we shared their quarters, of constantly rubbing shoulders with the Japanese.

A week after our arrival, several trainloads of rations arrived. A prodigious quantity of rice, salt, sugar, oil, and enough vegetables for thirteen hundred men had to be unloaded and stored. The first time a 220-pound bag of rice was deposited on my shoulders I simply crumbled. A Liverpool stevedore showed me how to arch my back and tense my abdominal muscles, and I discovered for myself the reason for the Chinese coolie trot and the mincing steps. Even the medical officers were roped in, and when the guards started hitting those unequal to the task, I went to see Saito, the lieutenant in charge of the camp. Saito just laughed and told me to get on with the job.

The food instantly improved, but out of sheer malice, rather than allow us the vegetables we needed, the Japanese held them back and let them rot.

NINE

(1943)

The trains pulled right into the middle of the camp. They came from Ronshii, and they always arrived at night. A great pyramid of wood was in readiness, and set ablaze. By its light we unloaded the sick from the open goods cars. They numbered around three hundred in each batch.

The journey had been hard on them. On some stretches they had to detrain and walk several miles, carrying their kit. In the wagons they were bundled up, shoulder to shoulder, lying down or sitting up. There was no protection from the rain, and for the last twenty-four hours they had been given no food. In every truck there was at least one dead man.

Those incapable of walking were taken off in makeshift stretchers. The others were helped to line up so that by the light of a candle they could be counted. A hot meal was ready in the huts.

The hospital was run along new lines. A combatant officer, not an M.O., was in charge of each hut. Huge efforts were made to keep everyone clean, although it was impossible to control scabies and lice. The fit and semi-fit were immediately organised into sanitation, wood collecting and cremation squads.

The man primarily responsible for bringing energy and confidence to the Tambaya camp was the senior medical officer. Bruce Hunt was an Australian major (before the war he had been a doctor in Perth) in whom physical courage was matched by moral steadfastness. His energy fuelled a natural capacity for planning and organisation. He had, in short, the prime qualities of leadership. Of medium height, broad shouldered, strong featured and almost completely bald, he exuded a taurine strength. Unfortunately, he also possessed the characteristics of the bull-in-the-china-shop: head down, he demolished any status quo he disapproved of, trampled reputations, and used physical violence when he thought it necessary. Unless checked, he could at times bring chaos to the order created by his own abilities.

The Japanese only saw in Hunt the opposite of all that is held dear to the military mind – discipline and loyalty. It might, of course, seem strange, even quite unrealistic, for our captors to expect our fealty. By the light of their understanding, however, the moment we had surrendered to them we had *ipso facto* inserted ourselves into their societal system, more precisely into their military structure. At times, when they spoke to me on a personal level, they tried to explain the notion of *gimmu*. In the complicated panoply of obligations and their reciprocals that penetrate Japanese life at all levels, *gimmu* represents the repayment of a debt that could by definition never be repaid completely. In our particular case, of course, the gift of life, the life the I.J.A. had magnanimously spared when we surrendered.

Virtue consisted in the right execution of duty (for which the word is *nimmu*), and on showing proper subservience to all above us. At the very top lived the Emperor. So low were we, and so removed from the Presence, that the transcendental power that issued from His Majesty couldn't reach us. Accordingly, we were exempt at dawn from facing in the direction of the Imperial Palace in Tokyo and, like all I.J.A. personnel, rendering homage and renewing allegiance. We possessed one option only, that of fitting in our P.O.W. role and of accomplishing our duty. This might have been an echo of the old Confucian precept according to which a servant is a better man who fulfils his duties more faithfully than his master executes those assigned to him by his rank.

More than once Hunt had been punished for failing to fit in the P.O.W. mould. On one occasion during the march, the prisoners had been herded into huts recently evacuated by coolies suffering from cholera. Hunt had courageously protested. His manner, however, had been too forceful and the argument presented in the wrong way. In the ensuing beating his left hand was broken.

Saito, a wartime officer and the Tambaya camp commandant, had clashed several times with Hunt. Secretly, I think, he admired him. Perhaps he was envious of his courage. Openly, however, he showed every sign of disliking him, and never let an opportunity pass without letting him know it. Once, as I was translating for

Major Hunt, Saito, who was in a mood for needling me as well, said: "That won't do at all, interpreter. You must study Nippon-go much harder. I don't understand a word of what you're trying to say."

I turned to Hunt and suggested that, as Saito refused to understand my Japanese translation, he, Hunt, had better speak to him directly. Saito understood English perfectly and spoke it with ease.

"No, no," said Saito in English, "I don't understand Major Hunt. He speaks Australian. I still need you to translate."

Hunt went pale. A short while back, he had explained to me that he found the Australian accent distasteful. He cultivated a smooth, rounded speech, close to what was then known as an Oxford accent.

Saito was erratic and unpredictable (bad officer material, as they said in the British Army). He allowed his men to mistreat us as they fancied. He couldn't even be bothered to check them, as we had requested, when they intruded into our quarters, disrupting our rest, borrowing and often never returning the few objects we still owned and that they envied.

Saito's mental circuits were mysterious. He produced associations which, to us, were incomprehensible. When, for example, Hunt requested that beans be included in our rations (they were, we had heard, in oversupply five kilometres south of us, at another hospital camp), Saito answered by deploring the effects of a liberal education. As a consequence of such an education the Allies, he went on to say, were venal and decadent. Major Hunt listened calmly as I translated with some difficulty the words that described a world far removed from the realities of a P.O.W. camp.

"Sir," said Hunt at last with some grandeur, "I am not interested in the merits or demerits of a liberal education. I've come here to get beans for my patients."

"*Kiotsuke!* Stand to attention!" screamed Saito, "I'm going to slap both of you!"

We snapped to attention. Hunt screwed his face into an exaggerated look of surprise. I said we never intended to be rude, simply that it was a doctor's duty (*nimmu*) to try and help the sick. Saito walked off.

We had not, however, heard the last of the blitz on liberal education; a few days later Saito came after dark into the officers' hut and started on an expanded version. The conclusion was, once more, a surprise. "I know that you say this railway is a present for Churchill. It is better in life to live with the truth than with the things of the imagination. I must disillusion you absolutely: Churchill will never have the railway."

Hunt's energy and courage produced results: we got our beans, and Tambaya ran more smoothly and efficiently than any other camp we'd ever been in. That it wasn't a working but a hospital camp made, of course, a big difference.

Among the officers who dealt directly with the Japanese there was a Major T., whom I distrusted. I thought he was weak and pusillanimous. T. at the time acted as our quartermaster, the officer in charge of all supplies. His opposite number was a low-brow Japanese of Neanderthal appearance whom we had baptised Orang Utang (the two Malay words mean "man of the forest"). Orang Utang, a mere first-class private, was full of his own importance; in our presence he puffed himself up, a disdainful smile spreading over his face.

Major T. and Orang entertained a mutual antipathy. I wasn't much liked by either of them and found myself in the role of buffer.

There had been another beans conference with Saito, who had agreed to a slight increase. This apparently gave Major T. an idea when we went to see Orang at the Japanese cookhouse in order to draw rations.

"Ask him for more," he said.

I replied that if we did that we were more likely to receive a bashing rather than beans.

"Do as you're told, Sergeant," ordered T.

I did. A hefty smack landed on each cheek.

The same thing occurred a couple of days later. By then I had made Major T. understand that I didn't much enjoy interpreting for him, and he in turn would not speak to me except in the line of duty. He had, unfortunately, means of getting at me that I didn't possess.

"Tell him we need more beans," he said once again.

I asked him if he was aware of the consequences of such a request.

"What do you mean by that?" asked T. "It's an order. Speak up!"

Orang knew enough English to understand what was happening. He didn't wait for my translation. He swung his arms wide and his fists hit me right and left on the side of the head. My glasses flew off my nose and luckily landed unbroken on the ground.

Later I reported the incident to Colonel Hutchinson.

Hutch said, "All right, you don't have to tell me any more. Let's go and see the cadet."

Saito had gone off on leave and had been replaced by an officer cadet about whom we knew very little. He seemed innocuous enough in the few dealings we'd had with him so far.

The cadet was taking his new role seriously: he was booted, the collar of his tunic was tightly buttoned in spite of the heat, and he was wearing his cap when we found him seated in front of his hut, staring at the sky.

We bowed and explained that we had a *chotto mondai*, a little problem.

"*Nanda?* What is it?" he asked curtly.

Hutch explained. I felt awkward because the incident concerned me, and I didn't want the cadet to think I was whining. I tried to make Hutch's remarks as impersonal as possible, placing the whole matter on the plane of principles. Hutch's argument was that I was merely the interpreter and that it was wrong to punish me when the culprit was Major T.

For "wrong" I used a common Japanese word, *damé*, meaning "bad, inadequate." It was a word used constantly by the Japanese when speaking to us. Now, however, I was using it on them.

The cadet stood up slowly, stared at us and became very still. His upper lip started to tremble. Sweat broke out on his forehead, beneath the cap with the yellow star. His jaw shook and a scream came out of his mouth. "Bring me my sword!"

A private rushed off to the cadet's hut and brought back the sword. The cadet seized it and unsheathed.

He started ranting incomprehensibly. Froth bubbled on his lips. His legs jerked as if an electric current was passing through them. Clearly, he was out of his mind.

In a strangled voice he shouted, "Kneel! Heads down!"

I translated the order. Hutch and I sank to our knees and bowed our heads, not wishing to look at the cadet's face, and involuntarily baring our necks. The cadet swung his sword above me. The blade sliced through the air with a silky sound.

"The enemy soldiers I have killed with this sword!" he screamed. "Now you!"

I noticed with surprise that I felt no fear, but that I had withdrawn completely from the outside world. Thoughts rushed into my brain with such speed that they seemed to coalesce into one paramount imperative: I must die thinking a noble thought.

I glanced around me. This was my last sight – jungle, huts, Japanese, booted legs. There was nothing noble about that. I thought of God: and dismissed the notion immediately as abstract, entirely theoretical, fictitious even. I tried to conjure up the image of my parents: an impossibility, as surprising as the failure to review my whole life, such as we have been told happens when death is at hand.

Desperately searching for the noble thought that would enter my head just before it separated from my body, I evoked the image of England and the King; of beauty and of a girl I had loved; of art. Nothing worked. Everything was rubbishy, insubstantial. It had not the slimmest reality.

The mind suddenly emptied and went quiet. The uncontrollable "noise" of the neurons dragging with them random images extracted from the memory, even that ceased. The "monkey in the mind", to use the Indian expression, had stopped jumping around.

The truth then exploded as a voice never heard before and yet completely familiar: You are nothing. You have never thought or felt or said anything of value. You have been aping and parroting. You were given life for two decades, you were given your chance. Now you will die without leaving the slightest trace: not even that of an earthworm, not even a peep from a bird's throat.

I felt unspeakable desolation. I didn't understand why none of this had become obvious long ago. Didn't understand my blindness.

The cadet raised his sword. "What do you say before I kill you?"

"*Wakarimasen*. I don't understand."

The sword arm remained taut for an instant. Then fell slowly.

A thought flooded my brain: I am saved. I will live. Instantly I started trembling, a quiet and interminable tremor. I looked at Hutch, trying to turn my head as little as possible. His face was ashen. My head still down, I noticed that the booted legs had stopped twitching. The point of the sword was resting on the ground. Slowly I looked up. The cadet was immobile. The eyes were staring ahead, the mouth still, flecks of foam stuck at the corners. He looked down at us.

"*Ike!* Go!" was all he said.

"We can go," I said to Hutch.

We stood up, bowed and walked away.

We kept silent. From time to time Hutch grunted. Eventually I allowed myself to say that it had been a close shave.

"I'd rather call it a near miss, if you don't mind," Hutch remarked. He looked at me. "Something I want to tell you. I've told no one so far. Fact is I've managed to keep a small flask of brandy in my kit. Now's the time to have a go at it, don't you think?"

Later, as we were nearing the P.O.W. lines, Hutch said, "Better not tell anyone what happened. If Major Hunt hears of it he's liable to go and attack the cadet single-handed."

We surreptitiously pulled at the brandy flask, and retired to our respective huts. It was around five in the afternoon. We needed to recover.

I was shaken by the experience of coming close to death. The emptiness I had sensed was unlike anything I had ever learned or experienced. It had the strength of revelation. None of the haphazard cultural baggage I had acquired could accommodate it. How I would deal with it in the future, I had no idea. All I knew was that the next time I faced death there would have to be a trace – as visible as the earthworm's, as loud as the peep of the bird.

It was clear that the cadet had been the victim of a fit known as *musekinin*, a particular flaw in the central nervous system of the Japanese. *Mu* is the negative form used in a compound word; and *sekinin* simply means responsibility. The whole word, however, has a more specific meaning than "irresponsibility". It describes the loss of control we had just witnessed, almost a state of possession. Old Padre Andrews had his own ideas about it. It could have been inherited, he thought, from the Malay blood which forms part of the genetic cocktail that went to make the inhabitants of the Japan Archipelago. The Malays are known to suffer from singular dysfunctions of the nervous system. One, *amok*, is familiar: the afflicted person tries to murder everyone around. Another only affects old men who imitate all the gestures enacted in front of them. (When the British arrived in Malaya they put a stop to a favourite game of small boys; pretending to stab themselves in front of an old man, they handed him a knife which he would plunge into his chest). *Musekinin* was a variant of *amok*, explained Padre Andrews, who also had a theory concerning the elaborate code of verbal politeness of the Japanese language: it might well serve, he said, as a screen behind which the speaker could retreat in case he had inadvertently pushed the *musekinin* button.

The word *damé*, in my case, had clearly been the button. What had defused the situation, however, hadn't been a sleight of language. The script, in the cadet's mind, called for the abject and cowardly prisoner to beg for mercy; and for his head to be chopped off with the ceremonial sword. What tore up that script was my unexpected and irrelevant answer to his question, along with the absence of fear (fear, a defence mechanism, only appeared when the clinical signs of *musekinin* abated and hope was restored). The play had to stop.

Evening had fallen when a guard came to my hut with the order that Colonel Hutchinson and I were to report immediately to the cadet. I went to tell Hutch, who was working on his racing papers: Hutch knew by heart all the Derby winners since 1900 but he had more difficulty with other classic races such as the St Leger and the Thousand Guineas. "Hope he hasn't changed his bloody mind," Hutch said.

Once again, in silence, we made our way to the Japanese lines. At the door of the cadet's hut, we bowed. The cadet was seated on his sleeping platform, wearing only his *fundoshi*, a white g-string with a flap of cotton folded over the private parts. In front of him had been set out a candle stuck in a hollow bamboo; cakes and cigarettes; and a bottle of sake with three glasses.

"*Komban wa*, good evening, Colonel, good evening Mister Interpreter," said the cadet. "Please join me."

We kicked off our clogs and climbed on the platform. Sake was poured and cigarettes lit. We drank to our respective health, and to the recovery of the patients in hospital.

"Are you married, Colonel?" asked the cadet.

The Japanese were always curious about our marital customs. In reality they were passionately interested in contraceptives, banned by law in pre-war Japan where it was said that a liberal was someone who believed in contraception. As Hutch was married but didn't have children, in the past he'd been asked such questions as Was it his fault? Was his wife barren? And if not, what did they do not to have babies?

In order to spare him this kind of ordeal I had invented a family. I answered the cadet by saying that Hutch had two sons: one who went to Winchester and would surely become a servant of the state; while the other at Wellington wanted to follow his father's footsteps and go in for soldiering. It was explained that these two public schools were the traditional training grounds for the Civil Service and the Army.

The cadet made a slight bow and hissed, a sign of respect. "I see, Colonel," he said, "that you are devoting your two sons to the service of your country. There is no more noble destiny." Hutch made a deprecatory gesture and gave me a look in which I fancied I detected a sign of gratitude.

We talked about the value of a sovereign as opposed to an elected president, as in America; the cadet tried to imagine how the world would look after the war under the aegis of Japan; he described the kind of work we would be given (lighter than railway building); he even ventured to think that in the course of time we might be repatriated.

As the level of the sake bottle was coming down, and the cigarette pack was down to three, I nudged Hutch and suggested we take leave of the cadet. Hutch nodded. I bowed, mumbling about it's getting late, how grateful we were for the invitation, and how I trusted we had not bored the cadet. All this was a strain for me as I was desperately lacking in the niceties of social talk in Japanese. But the cadet accepted it all, bowing and hissing us out.

Discussing it later, Hutch and I decided that the party was a way of apologising for the afternoon's near-miss, and a plea not to say anything to Saito on his return from leave.

Hutch's remark about Hunt on the way back from the afternoon's "incident" hinted at a situation that was soon to come out in the open: the two men were struggling for the leadership of the camp.

Hutch was the *de jure* commanding officer, but Hunt's courage and initiative made him highly visible, almost conferring on him a hero's role. Not even the occasions when he used his fists on a prisoner whose attitude displeased him could diminish his stature. Often the man fought back. It certainly was an unusual sight (as well as an entertaining one in a gruesome way) when a major and a private engaged in a dogfight. Hunt generally came out the winner.

As for Hutchinson, it must have been Englishmen of his mould for whom the French invented the expression "perfidious Albion". Anyone taking a look at Hutch saw a stooped, bald and unmilitary figure who shuffled along with the help of a bamboo staff. His legs were knobbly and bowed. Their top half was hidden by floppy shorts that almost hid his knees. He appeared vague. He was a prize mumbler. He didn't speak much, and when he did it mainly concerned racing. It would clearly be child's play to try and bamboozle him. The truth was otherwise: Hutch was an excellent soldier and an astute man. He had been perfectly chosen as G-1, the officer in charge of intelligence for his brigade. Having at the beginning of our captivity made it possible for me to learn Japanese, he requested, once I had achieved a certain fluency, that I give him daily lessons in the language. He learned fast, but in our dealings with the Japanese he never let on that he understood a single word of what was being said. His knowlege, however, gave him two distinct advantages: time to think out an answer while I translated what, in most cases, he had already understood; and the ability to check me on those occasions when I took too much liberty in shaping his answers to make them fit the Japanese mentality.

Hutch no doubt admired what Hunt had achieved. We were, however, almost entirely in the power of one individual, the Japanese camp commandant: our lives depended on his good will, and Hunt had alienated every Tambaya camp commandant.

It was up to Hutch to try and repair the breach in a dangerous situation, and one which eventually would necessitate Hunt's removal as senior M.O. And we were naturally much relieved when at the end of September, Saito and his goons were replaced by a new guard under the command of a Lieutenant Eraiwa.

Eraiwa looked stern and sullen while Saito was showing him round the camp, prancing about in an unmilitary manner. The first encounters between him and us were glacial, and he made it very clear that he wouldn't stand for the nonsense his predecessor had put up with. He probably believed that we were made of the same stuff as Saito, although he soon noticed that the camp was well run. His attitude changed, and both sides felt a friendship fostered by mutual respect. The men under Eraiwa's command, without exception, were the best guards we'd ever had. They showed us as much courtesy as they did their own comrades. Only two men were ever hit. One was Colonel Dillon, who was visiting us, and once again the fault lay with Major T., my near nemesis, endangering a fellow prisoner through his stupidity. Unfortunately I have completely obliterated the details of the incident. My diary fails to mention exactly what happened, but states that T. got beaten up for his troubles. I must, in any case, have derived a good deal of satisfaction from knowing that T. had got his condign bashing. I'm equally certain that my satisfaction was tempered by the fact that the admirable Dillon had suffered unnecessarily.

From the period of Eraiwa's command I have, on the other hand, an acute memory of a specific encounter.

Eraiwa occupied the partitioned end of a long and narrow hut where his men also lived. He was seated on his sleeping platform when I entered. As I bowed, I saw in the men's section, through an opening in the partition, a sight which mesmerised me – the word is not too strong. The branch of a tree, four or five feet long, was hanging on one of the walls. Because of its shape, it instantly evoked an ideogram written by a master. Although incarnating repose, it projected a dynamic strength. Neither leaves nor small shoots impaired its linearity. In colour it was an even pale grey. Finally, its placement on the plane of the wall had been perfectly chosen.

A devil sprang up in me, almost a fit of jealousy; another tribe, an enemy tribe at that, had achieved what I perceived to be an extraordinary work of art, *objet trouvé* though it was. However, in the moment I wasn't quite as lucid as it would appear: that came later. The devil hid under a more acceptable form, a disdain for such tomfoolery. I turned to Eraiwa and asked him what "that" was. I could hear bitterness in my voice.

"This morning," he answered very calmly, very slowly, "two of my men went for a walk in the forest. They found this branch, and they hung it in their part of the hut in order to refresh the spirit of their comrades."

I bowed again when I left. Because I had to, and out of respect for Eraiwa's lesson.

Men were dying in ever increasing numbers. At one time dysentery would account for as many deaths as all the other illnesses combined. A few weeks later, unaccountably, beri-beri or ulcers would become the killer. Everyone, fit, semi-fit or patient, suffered from tertiary malaria. Hardly anyone recovered from the cerebral strain. As "key personnel" I received my regular dosage of quinine or atebrin but I was never free of fever for more than a fortnight at a time.

Dysentery by itself was not necessarily a cause of death, but its corollary, starvation, was. On Major Hunt's instructions, orderlies made sure that every patient finished the food that was put in front of him. It was a torture that started at eight a.m. when a pint of cold, maggotty rice accompanied by a bean soup had to be got through, spoon by spoon. By noon when it was consumed, another pint of the same nauseating stuff was brought to the patient. Yet the time came when a man with dysentery, however determined to survive, could not bring himself to eat any more: within a month he died.

In Tambaya ulcers were not as prevalent as in the working camps. But often, as the gaping wound spread and necrosis set in, only amputation could save the patient.

A broken-down hut that had once served as the rice-store was cleared of rubbish and disinfected as best we could with a hand spray. A crude bamboo operating table was built in the centre. The only surgical instruments we possessed were an incomplete set of post-mortem tools. They were boiled outside the hut.

Whenever an amputation was being planned I went to the Japanese cookhouse and borrowed the hand-saw. "See to it that it's clean when you return it!" the head cook always warned with a laugh, pleased with the quickness of his wit. The guards crowded around the operating table, relishing the sight of a man having his leg sawn off under these terrible conditions. A small quantity of ether was the only anaesthetic available. But that too eventually ran out.

The amputees knew that their chances of survival were one in ten. They were always asked whether they wished to undergo the operation, and their answer was almost invariably yes. They lay together in a small section of a ward, with no more than a blanket between themselves and the bamboo floor, without special food, without painkillers. They fought for life, in vain most of the time.

In October, we heard that a Japanese medical colonel would be visiting the hospital. A horror show was arranged. The most spectacular cases of emaciation, the largest ulcers, the bloated wet beri-beris and the amputees were carefully arranged at the edge of the sleeping platforms for the maximum effect. As soon as the colonel was announced, rags and banana leaves that served as dressings were peeled off. The show was a success. The colonel was impressed. Repeatedly he mumbled, *"O kinodoku, desu ne?"*, literally, "Honorable Spirit of Poison, isn't it?", meaning simply, What a shame!

By the end of the inspection tour we had great hopes. The colonel would surely help us. But all he said was that "until the real drugs arrive" he would advise us to treat dysentery with the charcoaled bones of bullocks, and ulcers with parboiled banana leaves.

Two great events happened that month.

On the 17th, the two rails, one from the north, the other coming from the south, met at Konkuita. The whole line, 263 miles long, with its 688 "bridges" (counting the large steel and wood structures along with those that just crossed rivulets) was operational.

A great celebration took place at the meeting point, and a day of rest was proclaimed for all prisoners and coolies. At Tambaya, everyone received one KOOA cigarette.

The railway line ran right through the camp, and we sat all day watching the inaugural trains roll by. There was in fact only one inaugural train, carrying staff officers and a brass band in its open carriages draped with bunting. The prisoners nursed their KOOAs, and took a certain pleasure, if not a secret pride, when they saw the result of their work. Involuntary though it may have been, still we felt it was in great part our blood that was responsible for this achievement. The second train carried war supplies. Knowing that they were destined for the Indian front, we saw them roll by with less pleasure. But when the third and last train of the day arrived, loaded with Korean prostitutes, prudery joined indignation: "Blimey! It's for these bleedin' whores that we built the railway!"

It was also that month that six hundred men under Colonel Hingston arrived without warning. They were accommodated with much difficulty. Although many were to die shortly, there were enough semi-fit among them to help with the fatigues. They were a welcome addition.

Among them were a handful of Dutch prisoners. One afternoon as I was sitting admiring the clear sky, and the open landscape with its graceful palm trees, a deputation of four Dutchmen came to see me. They were in rags and bearded. One of them asked me to confirm that I was the camp interpreter. He then introduced his companions: one was a rabbi. The rabbi addressed me in Yiddish. I said I was sorry but I didn't understand him. The next question was in English: "Are you Jewish?" When I gave an affirmative answer, the rabbi shot out something which was translated as "So what kind of a Jew are you? Speaking Japanese and not Yiddish?"

The deputation informed me that the Day of Atonement, Yom Kippur, was coming soon. Would I ask the Japanese to let them off duty and allow them to hold a service in public?

I said, no, I would not do so. Most Japanese, I explained, were admirers of the Nazis, and these Dutch Jews would be putting their heads in the noose. I also didn't see why they couldn't celebrate Yom Kippur privately, and why it was necessary to advertise it.

Of course, the argument was nonsensical, and it was uttered on the spur of the moment. It took hardly a moment's reflection to understand that in that remote corner of Burma childhood phantoms had unexpectedly appeared. These fearful phantoms had brought back the struggle with my authoritarian father and the revolt against stultified ritual.

Eraiwa and his men were relieved by another platoon of the same company under the command of Lieutenant Takeuchi. In their attitude towards us neither subaltern nor their troops differed much, and the change was imperceptible.

Not for Major Hunt, however. The new camp commandant fanned his quarrelsomeness even more than had his two predecessors. The climax came as a result of the scarcity of water; when the monsoon stopped, the little stream that ran at the side of the camp dried up, and so had a rivulet further on. There was a well nearby and we had used it without authorisation. A first class row ensued, stoked up by the mutual dislike of the two officers. Hunt and I were standing outside Takeuchi's hut. Takeuchi himself was hanging out of his window, loath to let Hunt enter his quarters. After some sharp words, Takeuchi ordered Hunt to be off. Turning to me, he said he would not have anything to do with him in the future.

Hutch had no option than to promote Major Phillips to the post of senior M.O. He let a few days pass and informed Hunt of the fact, making him believe that the order came from Colonel Banno. No one dared imagine what Hunt would do if he knew the truth.

A profound apathy once again set in. Unlike at Sonkurai, where James Mudie was operating his radio, in Tambaya we were completely ignorant of what was happening in a world increasingly unreal, the world at war.

The death curve rose. A few men went off their heads and had to be chained to trees. A patient escaped and some days later was recaptured in Anan Kwin, a neighbouring village. He was interrogated by Takeuchi, but he was incoherent and we pleaded insanity. He received a light sentence, a few weeks of local detention.

Although not as prevalent as in the working camps, the incidence of crime rose. Every effort was made to put down theft. As self-respect had widely vanished, we resorted to physical punishment and public humiliation. The culprit was taken out of his hut, and in front of his comrades bared his buttocks to receive a number of strokes administered with a thick bamboo. A record of his crime was taken down, and a prison sentence passed with the formal assurance that if the culprit survived the war, he would serve it in the Glasshouse, the infamous military detention centre at Aldershot.

The food deteriorated once again to rice and beans. We needed proteins. A Burmese cart driver arrived with a sick yak. I spoke to Takeuchi who allowed us to buy it. Hutch awarded me any part of the animal I fancied. Much as I had disliked liver all my life, that's what I now most craved. I devoured a small piece with relish, imagining a heavenly manna entering my body and enhancing life.

Another "coup" I managed to pull off was receiving permission for Major Price and myself to go to Thanbyuzayat and buy hospital supplies with a fund established from the officers' pay, considerably higher than ours. Takeuchi allotted us a lorry and one of his drivers. He never asked us to give our parole. It went without saying that we wouldn't escape. We had an unspoken understanding: we were "between gentlemen".

We left on November 23 in a holiday spirit. Alone, bouncing in the back of the lorry (Major Price was in the cab with the driver), I was unexpectedly reminded of my early childhood, of the summer journeys to Normandy, and the ineffable happiness I experienced looking out of the train window.

A road ran parallel to the railway track, but ten kilometres from the town we had to stop. A bridge was down and we negotiated an improvised causeway, recently built across the paddy fields. Together with two other trucks trying to get through we got bogged down, and it was night by the time we managed to extricate ourselves. We raced through Thanbyuzayat, and beyond the town we entered a large Japanese camp. Under the British it had been a Public Works Department coolie line, and until recently half of it had been occupied by Australian P.O.W.s; seventy had been killed in a recent air raid.

Eraiwa's platoon sergeant at Tambaya was on duty when we arrived. He gave us "a marvellous welcome", according to the diary. He would do everything for our comfort. We were shown our billet, a barrack room where twelve men due soon to return to Japan were well on the way to getting very drunk. A one-star private brought us food, drink and blankets, and everything would have been fine had we been able to go to sleep.

A violent discussion was under way. All giving voice in unison, different speakers were airing their opinions on how soon the I.J.A. would reach Delhi; reaffirming and reiterating their faith in the Emperor; and disputing some esoteric aspects of Shinto, the ancient cult of Japan. Furious spitting, thumping of fists, and throwing empty bottles of beer and sake emphasised key points.

Price and I were cowering under our mosquito net, trying to stay out of the *melée*, when in total darkness ("Lights Out" had just sounded on the bugle) a man reeking of drink joined us. Blowing his sake breath in our faces, he explained how the soul of Nippon is animated by the spirit of Bushido, the "way of the warrior". However, one of his companions dissatisfied with his exegesis, joined him under our net. A violent argument commenced, soon reinforced by blows. Several were stopped inadvertently by Price and myself, the legitimate occupants of the sleeping space.

I didn't wish to be thought a spoilsport; I also knew how the Japanese viewed drunkenness: if they didn't exactly condone it, they considered it with bonhomie and amusement. My fear was that our visitors might be horribly sick on the blankets. I went to get the Guard Commander, who dragged the two zealots to a cell. There, no doubt, they resumed their exchange of views without disturbing the hon. foreign guests.

Around three a.m. the bugle woke us up. It signalled the recruits to fall in on the parade ground in full service marching order, that is fully dressed, booted and putteed; and equipped with pack, rifle, bayonet and entrenching tools. N.C.O.s, roaring like bulls, were corralling their squads, and chivvying the men who rushed about in a state of terror verging on panic. They fell in, forming fours. There was no inspection: in the darkness, it would have been impossible. But the men in the last row of four, that is the last to fall in, were punished for being the slowest. The duty sergeant major stood in front of them, bawled them out and hit the front man with his fist. The blow fell square on his face. Forbidden to move his legs (he was standing at attention), the front man fell backwards, pulling down, like so many skittles, the three behind him. The parade was then dismissed.

This close and unexpected view of Japanese military life to a degree reconciled us to our status as P.O.W.s. Fear and brutality were the key to training. The One Star men were very young recruits, and so cowed that at meal queues, or at the canteen, they made room for us. For us, prisoners in rags! Their food seemed even worse than what we were getting in P.O.W. camps.

Price and I were privileged; the cook had also been at Tambaya. The old boy network functioned admirably. We were told never to eat the One Star privates' food, but to slip quietly to the back of the cookhouse where we received chunks of meat and double helpings from the cooks' private stewpan. The recruits, on the other side, were filling their mess-tins with greasy water and boiled pumpkin.

Lightheaded with freedom, we went into town. Thanbuyzayat had grown around its two streets: it was the busy railhead of the new line. We loitered in the bazaar, bargaining for *chatties*, earthenware bowls to use as bedpans, and eggs. No one seemed to be surprised when they saw us wander freely from shop to chop-house, neither the Burmese, nor the Indians, not even the Kempeitai, the dreaded field-gendarmerie, on duty at street corners. The Indian shopkeepers said yes, how sorry they felt for us; how they hated the Japanese; and how impossible it was to reduce their prices by ever so little as the inflation robbed them of their profits.

We had arranged to meet our Tambaya driver at noon in a chop-house. But once in the bazaar we couldn't resist instant fulfilment. We discovered a dark and steamy place, smelling wonderfully of spices, curries and grilled meat. We took a seat at a table by ourselves. We ordered fried rice, prawns and eggs. And a beer.

The time came to pay and get out. The chop-house habitués had pratically stopped eating and drinking to watch us devour our meal. They were talking to each other in whispers. Conspiracy, intrigue, threat even, were in the air. I could feel it. We were almost certain to have a difficult time reaching the door. The moment we made a move there would be a rush for us, we would be overwhelmed, and we'd lose all our belongings. We looked very poor, but everyone in the little town must have known the purpose of our visit. Surely, the King of England or the Red Cross will have taken care of us. We must be carrying a lot of money.

Price agreed with my estimate of the situation. Encouraged in my intelligence evaluation, I pointed out a particularly nasty-looking Burmese, for certain a *dacoit*, an armed bandit, squatting by the door. He was carrying both a knife and a *parang* through his belt, and he would be the one, I guessed, who would trigger the attack. Our tactical decision was to stay close to one another and rush for the door the moment the bill was settled.

A servant girl who spoke a few words of English said, "No pay OK." No, that won't do, we must pay, we argued. "Man here," she said indicating with her finger the bandit squatting by the door, "he pay."

As we went by, and said thank you to the *dacoit*, he slipped a five-rupee note into my hand.

We started on the road back to Tambaya, but when we reached the broken bridge we saw that the causeway had sunk under the mud. It would be impossible to cross it. Before turning around, we had a cup of coffee, ate chappatis and smoked a cheroot in a small eating house at the foot of a hill. On the crest of the hill itself, a tall pagoda threw its gleaming gold pinnacle into the pale blue sky, and we could hear the sound of its bells in the breeze. The paddy was emerald-green, and red hills stretched out in the distance. With a full stomach life could again be idyllic.

We went back to Thanbyuzayat where we stayed for four days until the bridge was repaired. Extraordinary news awaited us in Tambaya: orders had been received that we were to move back to Kanchanaburi. And from there, to Singapore.

TEN

(1943)

We'd been hearing distant noises about a move for some weeks. Few paid any attention; we had often been deceived. But with time the rumour had become stronger, and now the return to Changi, "the acme of happiness, and the peak of our dreams" (to quote the euphoric and uncharacteristic words of the diary) was about to happen: from the jungle where we expected our ashes to be scattered, we were going home.

Three hundred of the sickest men at Tambaya were to be left behind. And for many others, travelling fifty in an open railcar, the five-day journey would prove fatal.

But it was also a fantastic journey. We crossed the small camps where we had stopped on the march up. Now they were towns of bamboo and atap, marshalling yards of importance. The railway followed the road on which we had suffered so much, and here and there we would recognise a place where we had almost given up. The line passed right though Sonkurai camp. A new bridge had been built and a huge cross on the side of the hill indicated where over a thousand men were buried. The line in its final stages had not been built by P.O.W.s. The Engineers' treatment had rendered us completely valueless as a working force.

(1979)

The sun is low when we leave the Apalon bridge. In the darkness, we stumble, stub our toes and twist ankles. Once or twice we lose the path and backtrack. When we get to Kyandaw, where we're spending the night, I'm haggard with fatigue, and my right knee is giving me hell.

Next morning, Aung Song finds me a ride in a bullock cart returning empty to the Three Pagodas Pass. Lulled by the rhythmic creaking of the wooden wheels, and rocked by the seesaw of the cart, I fall asleep.

Back in the Mon officers' house, I find an invitation from General Nai Schwe Kyin to join him. "I have learned," it reads, "that you have been travelling in Mon Liberated Territory. It would be an honour if you visited me at our secret H.Q."

It's early afternoon, a day later, when, after a four-hour trek we reach the camp, tucked away in a dip between hills. Orderly rows of atap and bamboo huts remind me of the old P.O.W. camps. Our arrival has been signalled, for the General is waiting to greet us at the gate. Behind him stand three young men. Only the General is wearing army uniform, or rather half-uniform; from the waist up it's jungle green combat shirt with belt, revolver and bolo knife; below the waist, it's a *longyi*, the Burmese sarong, heather and blue. The effect is very "war of liberation" style, no signs of rank, no decorations.

I meet the young men: Nai Rotsam and Nai Tala Mon, of the Central Committee; Nai Htaw Mon, Secretary of the Military Council. We go off for coffee and the first of several briefings.

The General was a petty officer on an Indian Navy minesweeper during the Second World War. After the departure of the British in 1947, the Mons took to the field and fought for a semi-autonomous status. But U Nu, the Burmese prime minister, first insisted on surrender.

The Mon People's Front struggled for ten years and then gave up, except for Nai Schwe Kyin, who in the meantime had spent three years in a Mandalay jail. "One man, one flag and no arms" was his motto at that time. He founded the new Mon State Party.

"Ne Win seized power in '62," he explains, "and his viewpoint was that as most of the Burmese have Mon blood, there was no need to give us ethnic rights. One of the historical reasons for Ne Win's attitude is that by royal decree in the eighteenth century, the Mons were obliged to call themselves *Talaings*. The word means bastard so they said No, we're not Mons, we're Burmese."

"We're four million in Burma, three in Thailand," he says later. His English is excellent. "We're widely dispersed and poorly integrated. We have seldom been dominant politically, but important economically and in the field of culture. We were good seafaring people: it was the Mons who started the Siamese Navy. Many admirals were Mons."

The commercial side is next heard. "Did you know," asks one of the Central Committee boys, "that the British wanted the Thais to pay them £125 million for your railway? If the Thais had agreed, I wonder whether you survivors would have seen any of it? But the Thais said no, and I can see why. So the Royal Engineers dismantled it! On our side, from Thanbyuzayat to the Three Pagodas, it was the Karens and the Mons who sold the rails."

Evening falls and a small march-past of one infantry platoon is laid on for me. At the General's right, I take the salute. "British drill, you will notice," says my host, smiling. He stands ramrod straight, a medium-size, compact man with a taut face.

The flag is brought down to the accompaniment of a bugle call and the presenting of arms. We walk back to the mess for dinner. The meaning of the flag is explained: the red background symbolises courage; the light blue star is the guiding North Star, the Mons' faith; and the golden sheldrake in the centre stands for harmony and unity: male and female fly in pairs, and if one is killed, the other refuses to fly alone.

The Chairman says goodnight and leaves with an armed escort. He sleeps in different houses, away from the camp, in case the Burmese Army mounts a night attack.

An assault exercise is laid on so that I can photograph Mon troops "in action". A truck arrives with supplies of arms and ammunition, not in the usual wooden boxes but wrapped up in white cotton to look like bales of cloth. Everyone present pitches in to help transport them to the armoury. The Chairman tells me that Mons living in America have been very helpful. He asks if I could help with the procurement of light weapons. Under his instructions, I write down the list: U.S.-made M-16s; German G-3s; M-79 grenade launchers; and M-72s, light anti-tank rockets. I know someone in Switzerland who is "dabbling in arms" and so I say perhaps, but payment must be in rubies, the famous Mogaung rubies. I know, however, that the Mogaung mines are in Karen territory. So perhaps a deal can be made with the Karens? The General says, "I'll look into it."

Before the return trip to the Three Pagodas, I'm taken to see the civilian side of the camp where mostly women are at work. The men are at the front, I'm told. Here they grow rice and raise ducks, pigs and fowl. In other Mon camps they also grow crops such as cotton, castor beans and sugar cane.

At the weaving centre, I'm presented with two *longyis*, a red and a blue. I take a last photograph of the Chairman. He shakes my hand.

"Thank you for coming," he says. "Tell the world what is happening to us. How we are fighting. And when we achieve our independence, there will be a villa on the coast near Ye for you to rest in your old age. Consider yourself an honorary Mon."

On the way back from the Three Pagodas I stay and rest for a week with Jacques Bes and his rafts. Aung Song sleeps almost without interruption for two days.

The two women from the French Embassy are back, along with a Belgian resident of Bangkok and his family.

I'm questioned. What did I find "up-country"; what was it like travelling with the guerillas; and what did I feel, going back to the places where I'd been a prisoner?

Yet I sense all the time that the questions are not so much about the journey itself, but about the way my experiences relate to already acquired knowledge, to official history, in effect to *The Bridge on the River Kwai*.

"Was it as bad as the movie showed it to be?" is always the first thing asked. I was one of the two technical advisers, and I'd spent two months in Ceylon, as Sri Lanka was known in 1957, where the film was shot. It was not unnaturally assumed that somehow I had injected my own truth into the script.

I reply that the reality was in fact much worse than anything seen on screen. One of the reasons was that David Lean, the film's director, didn't want to turn out an anti-Japanese tract, and he soft-pedalled all the horror bits.

But what seriously puzzles the Belgian is that Colonel Nicholson, the film's central character, is a turncoat; or, as he says, a Quisling, a collaborator. For it's thanks to Nicholson, the senior British officer in the camp, that the bridge is properly constructed (the original Japanese design was faulty); and when Allied commandos get ready to blow it up, in order to save what he now sees as his achievement, he openly sides with the Japanese. In the course of pursuing his obsession he finds it necessary to get the prisoners, the men under his command, to help him realise his project; to become, in other words, his blind but willing accomplices.

The meaning of Pierre Boulle's novel, the basis of the movie, changed fundamentally during its transformation into a film script. Boulle wanted to show the folly of man: more precisely the obfuscation of his ideals and the distortion of his goals.

Boule wrote in a memoir that the character of Nicholson was inspired by two officers he had known in Indo-China, who had sided with Vichy in 1941. Boulle, a Gaullist, was disciplined by these two men who considered him a traitor. Uppermost in their minds was the legitimacy of the Vichy government which, at the time, blinded a great many French to what were the real but distant interests of the country.

David Lean, who during the war was a conscientious objector, injected into the script an idea of his own, an idea which eclipsed Boulle's intention, and became the story's mainstay: simply, that in the military mind there necessarily exists an element of criminality. For Lean, the career of a regular army officer was a life of wrong-doing. Perhaps a life dedicated to evil.

It's in that light that Colonel Nicholson's actions can be understood.

Alec Guinness saw Nicholson differently: for him the man was simply mad. The difference in these two interpretations came into the full light of day, or in this case the full glare of the arc-lights, the morning David Lean directed the scene when Nicholson, like the Pied Piper, enters the sick men's hut, and urges the patients to follow him to work on the bridge.

Lean had explained to Guinness that he must look his actors directly in the eye, and deliver his speech forcefully: it was a deliberate, conscious order.

As the cameras roll, Guinness strides into the hospital hut, his swagger stick tucked under his arm, and stops in front of an extra clothed in rags and sitting on his sleeping platform. A faint smile appears on Guinness's face, he juts his chin up, and he directs his gaze above the patient's head. He has only just started speaking his lines when Lean orders "Cut!"

The camera rolls for Take 2, and Guinness repeats his performance exactly as before.

After Take 18, Lean slumps on a tree trunk, and takes his head in his hands. There's a long silence, then Lean looks up and says, "Alec, you win."

In all its important aspects, the movie is fiction. It's unimaginable that a British commanding officer collaborating with the Japanese wouldn't have been quickly demoted and removed by his fellow officers. It's hard to believe that a railway-building battalion of the I.J.A. would be incapable of building a perfectly serviceable bridge across a river a hundred yards wide, no doubt part of the delusion that science and technology are indissolubly associated with the white race. Lastly, although every important bridge on the Siam-Burma Railway was blown up, it wasn't Commando Force 316 that did the job but American and British air attacks. There was indeed a Commando Force (number 136!) operating in Burma close to the Thai border, but its role was to save P.O.W. lives in case of a general massacre, and to co-operate with the Free Thai forces.

As for collaboration, any head-on collison with our captors was folly, and a show-down suicidal. We were therefore obliged to engage in a quid-pro-quo which we hoped would eventually profit us. One way was to relieve the Japanese of certain onerous duties.

At Tha Markan, the steel bridge near Kanchanaburi, Lieutenant Colonel P.J.D. Toosey, determined to save as many of his men's lives as possible, made such a deal: he convinced the Japanese that the issue of tools, the allocation and planning of work, even the supervision of the prisoners at work, would be best handled by his own officers. The guards then would be responsible for precisely what their role indicated, the prevention of escapes. In order to establish the sort of *bona fide* that would be intelligible to the Japanese, Toosey (who was thought by many to be too "regimental", as our own Colonel Dillon was, and for identical reasons), instituted military pomp and panache as far as it was possible under the circumstances. The Japanese thought him an honourable man, much as Lieutenant Eraiwa did when he allowed Major Price and myself to go off to Thanbyuzayat without giving our parole. Colonel Toosey became a hero to his men, not a collaborator.

The French women say, yes all this is clear, but after all it's just a movie, it's an entertainment.

I agree. But Sam Spiegel, the producer, refused to say so in the credits, as he was requested to by ex-P.O.W. associations. The film is presented as a re-enactment of reality, and it's the film that remains in the public's memory.

The bridge at Kanchanaburi *is* the place where it all happened. Even altering reality there, it has been necessary to gild the lily: what appeared on the poster in the Bangkok railway station was not the steel bridge, but the wooden viaducts of Wampo, the better to conform to an imaginary bridge built by prisoners over a jungle stream.

I'm asked how I felt about being on the set of a P.O.W. camp.

It wasn't a happy time for any of us. In the jungle of Ceylon where a Danish company had built a wooden bridge, there were no entertainments, and only one woman in the crew, the script-girl. Moreover, we were convinced that the film would fail lamentably.

This was the first time I'd worked on a film set and I didn't know that movie-making is inevitably linked with infinite boredom. Even the busiest technicians only work intermittently.

For me, it was even worse. Once I had shot my key pictures for a *Life* magazine story, I had strictly nothing to do as David Lean wasn't in the least interested in my suggestions. My one and only serious contribution was the kapok-and-flint lighter situation. I could well imagine that a scene showing a prisoner/actor lying on his back and pumping a length of string tied to his big toe was so ludicrous that the sequence ended up on the cutting-room floor. It certainly never appeared in the final version of the movie.

The other technical adviser was Major General Lancelot Perowne, who had fought with Wingate's Chindits behind the Japanese lines in Burma. He was the specialist on commando operations, but his main use to David Lean was as crowd controller. Whenever extras had to march and look like British soldiers, Perowne was called to direct them on the set.

Physically Perowne was the archetypal major general. He was tall, whippet lean, moustachioed and very fit. We shared not only the same Cinghalese servant in the hut we'd been allotted, but feelings of frustration and dishonesty. We were being paid huge sums for contributing nothing.

One evening at dinner, Perowne turned to Lean.

"I say, David, can you spare John and me for a couple of weeks?"

"Absolutely, General," answered Lean.

"Then tomorrow could you release a Land Rover from the motor-pool?"

That is why, for a well-remunerated fortnight, the two technical advisers went roaming through the jungles and the tea plantations of Ceylon.

There isn't another film to come out of the Second World War that has had such success or such longevity. (Its First World War equivalent would be *All Quiet on the Western Front*.) Had it not been for the Lean/Spiegel film, the Death Railway would have been an almost invisible wrinkle in the history of the last World War. Apart from a few survivors and their families, hardly anyone would have ever heard of the Kwai, or to give it its real name, the Mae Nam Kwae Noi, or "Little Kwae".

It's also likely that much of the anti-Japanese feeling still found in Britain is a consequence of the film's wide exposure, precisely the opposite effect to what David Lean wanted.

(1943)

The two steam-engines, one pusher, one puller, puffed and wheezed up gradients, then stopped, exhausted. Those of us who could got out and walked up the hill. Out of consideration for the locomotives, the engineer might also request that we continue on foot to the next station. At other times, we ran out of fuel. Once more we jumped off our flatcars, roamed around the jungle, tearing down bamboo, gathering dead wood, and a couple of hours later a head of steam had been worked up. We were on our way.

Over the five-day journey we averaged three miles per hour.

At a stop we were joined by 150 coolies, men, women and children, all visibly sick. Yelling, the guards hit anyone moving too slowly, even the poor wretches dragging themselves on the ground. When they reached the two closed boxcars that had been shunted on to our train (the "ricetrucks" in which thirty of us had been jammed on the way to Banpong were now to enclose over twice our numbers), they were hoisted through the doors by a couple of British medical orderlies. These doors remained shut and locked for three days, the coolies forbidden to leave the wagons.

The scene was a recapitulation of the year gone by: the guards' screams, "*Kora!*", "*Baka Yaro!*", "*Speedo!*"; the sound of cudgels hitting flesh and bone; the coolies' cries; the unbearable stench of disease, and the unbearable sight of man's inhumanity.

At Nikki, our guards couldn't contain their lubricity when they saw, stopped on the track parallel to ours, a train filled with "comfort-girls", prostitutes on the way to Burma.

I wished one white-faced and rouged Japanese girl a happy trip. She bowed and put her hand up to her mouth as if to hide a smile. But we too, the prisoners, were moved; most of us hadn't seen a woman since Banpong.

The train stopped outside Kanchanaburi. We got off the flatcars in which we'd spent the last five days, and lifted out the men unable to move. They were laid on the ground, while the fit, walking sick and "gondoliers" formed a ragged column ready to move off. We would come back for the stretcher cases.

We must have seemed a pitiable rabble. An army staff car went past us and abruptly pulled up. A Japanese officer gaped at us through the open window. After a minute, he called out: was there anyone who spoke Nippon-go?

I was walking next to Hutch at the head of the column. With Hutch's permission, I went over to the car and saluted. The officer, a Kempeitai major, ordered me to sit next to the driver. Nothing was said during the ride to the major's office.

I was offered tea and I was asked: Who are you? What happened to you? Where do you come from?

The major handed me a sheaf of paper and three pencils.

"You give this to your commanding officer. I want him to write down the story of the past year. I want details. And names. You don't have anything to fear. Tomorrow I will send someone to pick up the report. Now my car will take you to the camp."

We named names. Toyama's among others. Later there were rumours that the Kempeitai had shot a number of the Engineers mentioned in the report. It was never proven and I doubted it. Anyway, Toyama surfaced later.

We remained two weeks in the Kanchanaburi camp. An amnesiac cloud hides all memories of that period with the exception of two unimportant and disconnected images.

The first is of breaking eggs into a blackened pan for a ten-egg omelette; and at the same time trying to keep my head out of the smoke, and feeling my eyes tearing.

The other is of leaving my tent at night for the fourth or fifth time for a trip to the latrines. One of my companions in the tent was a Rupert Brooke type, a private in the Malay Volunteers, and an Oxford double-blue, who had worked before the war for Jardine Mathieson in Hong Kong.

"You're at it again?" he asked irritably as I was disturbing his rest.

"Well," I said, "you remember poor Captain Oates who left his tent and said, 'I am just going outside and I may be some time'. A gallant man, Oates."

Double-blue was a terrible snob, but "up-country" his interest in the different hierarchies of society had somewhat abated. Now with food reviving us, life was returning to normal.

"Oates? What regiment is he in?" he asked, as I lifted the tent flap.

III

THEREAFTER

ELEVEN

Back in Singapore an anxious melancholia replaced the previous year's desolation as the months trickled away to our third P.O.W. Christmas. We grew anxious, because as the Allies came closer to victory, the closer we felt we might be approaching a fatal showdown with our captors.

In April 1944 all the P.O.W.s in Singapore were regrouped around the Changi Jail, except for the hospital cases who were sent to a new camp, Kranji, in the north of the island. The usual atap huts had been laid out in a rubber plantation adjacent to the road leading to the Causeway and the mainland. Hutch was posted as C.O., and I went along as his interpreter.

By a common and unspoken consent there was little talk of the year "up-country". A sense of propriety held us back from investigating the factors that had kept us alive, while so many fitter and worthier friends went under. It was luck, we said.

Yes, it was luck, or the accident of birth, if you were the right size. Too tall and too large, proportionately you received fewer calories than a smaller man. The Military Police, all six-footers and over, were among the first casualties. But if you were undersized, the hard physical tasks taxed you more than a larger man, and you went under faster.

Luck, if you had been fed properly as a child. There was a difference in the survival rate whether your family had been poor or well off; if you had been brought up with sweet tea and fish-and-chips, or on a diet of vegetables, fruit and proteins. Officers fared better than Other Ranks; men from county regiments better than those recruited in large cities.

Again, luck if you were at the right time of life. On the Death Railway the very young, lacking endurance, died first; followed by the men in their forties who lacked the natural power of recuperation found at an earlier age.

Nor could you do much to influence or control the existential factors: some camps were far preferable to others (Sonkurai, for obscure reasons, was, as we have seen, the worst); certain assignments could be hazardous, like rock blasting, or fatal, such as working in the river day after day; you could by mischance find yourself in a squad under the command of a sadist; or you might have all your belongings stolen.

But it was not just a matter of mere luck. There were other factors as well. Like everyone else in F Force I had my own ideas about ways to stay alive. At this great distance, however, I can't say which came to me on the Kwai, which in Kranji after my return, and which have accrued since. At the time, however, I had no doubt that my specific work had been the prime reason for my survival.

The most obvious factor was of course food: given the little we received and its low nutritive content, I had a far better chance of holding out than the men who worked on road and bridge twelve or sixteen hours a day.

Equally important was the nature of one's work. Unlike Colonel Nicholson in *The Bridge on the River Kwai*, opening up the jungle and building a railway gave us neither pride nor a sense of achievement. Our efforts were serving the military aims of the I.J.A., but there was a way (covert and immensely humble) to fight the enemy. It was to collect termites, and release them in the struts and pilings of the railway bridge we were building over the Huai Ro Khi at Sonkurai. We knew it was mere bravado, but it served to give our lives a semblance of purpose. We never found out if the stratagem was effective as the bridges were destroyed by aerial bombing long before the insects could prove whether they would collaborate.

Deprivation of a meaningful activity induced such a sense of worthlessness that it could lead to a state close to insanity. On two separate occasions a prisoner approached me with the request that I ask the camp commandant to accept his incorporation into the I.J.A. I started by describing the trials of a Japanese "one-star" man (the nightly parade at Thanbyuzayat provided lurid material), and continued with a recitation of the horrors awaiting a *Leiko*, an auxiliary such as our Korean guards, and typical of the treatment that any foreign-enlisted man could expect. My part done, I directed the unfortunate to one of the better padres.

My own work, I imagined, had a direct bearing on our relationship with the Japanese, and so indirectly could influence the well-being of everyone in camp. I saw my duties reach beyond the limits of a merely accurate translation. There were situations when an interpreter might advise a new approach; or, if the meeting was taking a negative and potentially dangerous turn, he might be called on to protect his superior by blaming his own inadequacy with the language.

Such an instance was Major Hunt's request for rice-polishings. At the time, more men were dying of beri-beri than from any other cause, and rice-polishings contain a high proportion of Vitamin B.

"If the horses of the Imperial Cavalry can have them, why can't the prisoners?" asked Hunt.

I never would have translated that remark. We could run into trouble on three separate counts. The first was the heavy-handed irony underlying the question. The second may be thought far-fetched, yet for mere prisoners to place themselves on an equal footing with the imperial steeds might be a form of *lèse-majesté*: who knows, these horses might also carry the Imperial Chrysanthemum on their harness. Thirdly, we were not *entitled* to anything. Consequently, requests had to be framed in a special way, the myth being that whatever we received was dictated by the compassion and generosity that the samurai code enjoined towards the defeated. (Unfortunately, there was nothing I could do to protect Hunt and correct the situation; the camp commandant was Saito, who understood English perfectly. Saito got very angry and slapped us both hard.)

The inherent difficulties of the language and the need to improve my performance kept me mentally alert. Emotionally, I was saved from sinking into a state of lethargy; instead of a mute and passive acceptance of orders, in every confrontation there was the possibility of manoeuvring, and sometimes of winning.

Even at my not very advanced or refined level of Nippon-go, I was vouchsafed a special insight into the Japanese character that others at a remove could not have. This insight was particularly rewarding when I was on my own and not translating for one of my superiors.

The basic and most frequent incident involved a guard beating up a prisoner for a real or imagined infraction of the camp rules. I had the choice of either accepting the offender's denial, and explain to the guard that it was a misunderstanding, an involuntary omission, an unfortunate mix-up. I could say that I knew the man personally, and he could never have lacked such respect as omitting to bow or salute. Or, if the accusation was one of illegal trading, I would appear astounded; the alleged offender was famous among the prisoners for refusing to have anything to do with the black market. If the guard knew and respected me, any of these lines might work and the incident was defused. Another approach was to counsel the accused to admit to his "crime"; and to pretend that I myself was so appalled by it that I would turn him over to "Rhino" for punishment. Often the guard would ask me to give up such a course of action; the prisoner's offence wasn't that bad! "Rhino" was the nickname we'd given to one of our regimental sergeant majors, a man of such ferocity in appearance, voice and deed that even the Japanese were awed by him. (He came to a bad end: on the ship that was taking him back home in 1945, one night he was seized on deck and thrown overboard by his own men.)

It was only under the extreme conditions of Sonkurai that I came to understand the advice I had been given in Singapore during the early days of our captivity. And with hindsight, it could well be that its importance in my survival was even greater than that of being an interpreter.

The words were those of a captain in his late forties who had worked in Malaya and been commissioned in one of the local regiments. One evening, after a game of bridge (this, remember, was Changi), he began reminiscing about his experiences in the First World War.

"Who knows where we'll be sent to," he said, "what's going to happen to us. Anyway, we'll be in the bag for a long time. I was taken prisoner by the Germans in '17, and I'm sure of one thing: it was a picnic compared to what's awaiting us. But remember: whatever happens, however dreadful the times you'll be going through, you've got to be able to say 'This is something I never would have had the chance of seeing before.'"

We looked at each other – the three young men who had been playing cards with the captain – no doubt each thinking, "What is he talking about? It's bad enough here in Changi."

It was necessary to draw nourishment from the circumstances, the captain said. Although they might seem unbearable, they were exceptional. As every day of our life was exceptional. So at the end of each day, it should always be possible to think back and recall, "Today, I have seen this, I have learned that."

"That's what will keep you going," he said. "Just now your heads are filled with hopes of returning home. But that won't last for ever. Memories of home will fade. Hope will thin out, become distant and unreal. It won't sustain you any more."

He was right. Deficiency didn't only apply to calories and vitamins. Pain and overwork drained a prisoner's psychic reserves; his will to live was whittled away, and the vacuum was filled by despair. The threads slackened that tied him to life, both past and present, and as his attention failed, he became more vulnerable to the stresses of a harsh and dangerous existence. "Give-up-itis" set in, and in most cases was irreversible. Death, anyway, was part of the day's events. For many, teetering at the edge of the decision, whether to fight or to give up, death was the escape from hopelessness. The prisoners died quietly. There was no fuss, no struggle to hang on to life, no calls for someone to be present at the extinction. It was a private and natural affair. The rites of passage were faced alone. Often, there was a smile on the lips of the moribund; they were about to find deliverance.

Everyone was aware how close we were to death, but few took a conscious decision: *Will I really do anything in order to survive? And by which means? What compromises will I accept?*

Those who said yes to the first question for the most part didn't have much success. A reason was needed. The mere will to stay alive wasn't sufficient. When all efforts were directed to the acquisition of food and the avoidance of strenuous work assignments, even if they were successful, the time came when there was no more point in pursuing the aim. The rewards were found wanting, and solace non-existent. The struggle was then abandoned.

The other two questions were answered by my old friend O.M. who, when he saw the disintegration of moral law in Sonkurai, said to me, "I don't know how to make my own rules. I won't start on that. All I think I can do is try to live like a Christian."

O.M. had never, to my knowledge, been a religious man, but I understood him and I could only acquiesce. Also I feared for him, and in that I was right for within a month he died. Unwilling to trade in the black market, to accept favours, to try and get light work, even to "scrounge" for extra food, he found himself among the most dispossessed. He became one of the prisoners who worked hardest and longest, and who received the least.

In between the two groups, those who would stop at nothing and the others who would never compromise, came the majority who feathered their nest as best they could without, if possible, raiding their neighbour's. They were the pragmatists, and some of them survived.

In Sonkurai, not many. When the camp was evacuated, of the 1,600 men who had arrived in May, only 400 returned to Singapore, eight months later. And by the war's end, there were only 182 left alive of the 400.

Discipline and *esprit-de-corps*, two components of the military glue known as morale, soon disintegrated in Sonkurai. But in the camps up the line where the Australians faced similar conditions the incidence of crime was much lower than in ours, and they suffered fewer casualties. Under stress they seemed more resilient than we were and better able to adjust to change. Another advantage was their greater physical endurance, as well as their familiarity with the hardships of outdoor life. Worse off than the British were the Dutch, while the coolies, bereft of any internal leadership, suffered most.

How prisoners fared in any given place depended on several factors. One was the image they projected, for the Japanese were extremely sensitive to signs. Not that signs replaced substance. Rather, they were its forerunner. Perhaps, in a hierarchical society welded to a set culture, it was necessary to signal at the same time one's proper place in the structure and the course of the action one proposed to take. Two signs could be expected from us. They would denote the prisoner's acceptance of his place in the world and the understanding of his duties, namely obeisance, observance of the rules and devotion to work. Yet if, over and above these signs, the Japanese saw indications that evoked for them "the way of the warrior", i.e. the virtues enjoined by Bushido, they were open to a change of attitude. The possibility then existed of overcoming our prisoner status, more specifically its shame and its degradation.

As we embodied these virtues, so we were treated. At the simplest level, we had seen how a semblance of military posture while on the food line at Tha-Khanun had been rewarded with extra rice. In a more complex way, Colonel Dillon, a professional in his own rigid and traditional system, instinctively understood the Japanese game and played it well. He dressed as neatly as he could; his Sandhurst stand (feet apart, spine slightly arched backwards) was always impeccable; and his moral courage was known up and down the line. Once, however, he overstepped the limits of the possible. It was in Nikki, a couple of days after his "dog" address, when he instituted parade-ground drills. The sight of men in rags, many barefoot, square-bashing in the mud under the dripping jungle canopy, to the bark of the N.C.O.s' "Mark Time! Eyes Right!", was bewildering even to followers of Bushido. Understandably, the prisoners' resentment was such that the exercise lasted only a couple of days.

Major Hunt, whose unorthodox and vigorous measures were admired by the prisoners, was, as we have seen, intensely disliked by the Japanese. Although they certainly didn't deny his courage, they found him lacking in samurai quality, of which the most important ingredient was loyalty. In our context, loyalty was above all respect for the I.J.A. The very source of Hunt's popularity with us rendered him ineffectual in his dealings with our captors.

An axiom of Dillon's was that without their officers, men perished, and he was probably right. But the truth was that survival was more often due to the existence of the military framework, than to the personal abilities of most of the officers I saw around me. Their mere presence did not save lives when the framework crumbled.

Because of my work, I found myself more in the company of officers than men of my own rank, and I was struck by the rigidity of their attitudes. Both regular and wartime officers were locked in a class system they could never renounce, even in circumstances when it was patently harmful; it was a system which, of course, reflected life in Britain.

The Other Ranks, to give just one example, greatly resented the officers' incessant representations to the Japanese concerning manual labour. True, the Geneva Convention (which the Japanese did not recognise) specified that they were exempt from it, but the officers' claim was that they would lose the men's respect, and hence their ability to command them, if they were seen to work side by side with them. (The compromise, made *in extremis*, was to agree to working squads made up entirely of officers!)

The O.R.s' considered view was that, regardless of rank, every fit man should be working on road or bridge, and leave camp fatigues, generally assumed by the officers, to the walking sick.

Such was the gap between commissioned and non-commissioned soldiers in the British Army of that period that in Tambaya, where relations based on mutual respect had been established between the Japanese camp commandant and the prisoner officers, a corporal once said to me, "You know, there's really more in common between the Jap lieutenant and our own officers than there is between them and us." He was right, and I sensed his secret humiliation. He had correctly perceived the common imprint that social code and manners leave on the upper stratum of human society. The imprint is found in all cultures and is unmistakable. It was one of the themes of *La Grande Illusion,* and nothing much seemed to have changed between the two wars. Nor, in fact, since Boswell: "Gentlemen of education, [Dr Johnson observed], were pretty much the same in all countries."

Although not of officer rank, I was always treated as if I had received the King's commission. Once, however, I had cause for resentment. The offender was not, as might be imagined, Major T. whose obstinacy had almost cost me my head at Tambaya (he was a fool), but the officer who stole "my" bed, for he was a knave. On the initial stages of the march, I had found, jettisoned by the side of the track, a canvas-and-metal camp bed, light in weight and of excellent design. I'd picked it up and carried it to the next camp. As I was about to complete its assembly, a lieutenant strode up to me, seized the bed, and walked away with it, grandly announcing, "It's mine." I went to his superior, and invoked the law of salvage at sea. "You're not in the Navy, and you're not to tell me what I'm to do, Sergeant. The fact that it was thrown away doesn't make it yours."

The outstanding officers were generally found among men with a vocation, doctors and chaplains being the most obvious examples. Few of us at the time knew anything of James Mudie's efforts and devotion to operating the radio he had sucessfully concealed during the Kempeitai search in Banpong. Almost daily, Mudie and his team listened to broadcasts from Delhi and news of the Allies' progress. However slow the advance, whatever the reverses, it didn't matter. Above all else, the radio helped maintain a feeling of connection, even if it was strictly one-way, with the outside world. It was our incomparable morale booster.

In Sonkurai, as the officer in charge of the cremation party, working between the cholera hill and the funeral pyre, Mudie wasn't likely to be much visited by the Japanese. The problem of electrical supply was solved when a truck limped into camp and, because of the road condition, would have to remain in Sonkurai until the monsoon abated. Mudie's team offered to assume its maintenance; they would keep it in good repair, which, of course, necessitated running the engine regularly. The Japanese gladly accepted the offer. The well-charged battery was daily taken out of the truck, hidden in six-gallon food containers and brought to the cremation hill.

So effective and safe was the scheme that often the battery wasn't replaced until a new charge was needed. One of the minor problems, however, was the aerial that was occasionally knocked down by wild elephants. These elephants were males who roamed around the camp at the period of rut or *musht*, attracted to the females that worked alongside us in logging operations.

I'd always had an affinity with elephants, and now I observed the intelligence and the delicacy these huge animals would apply to moving a tree trunk that had got jammed in a gully, or to disentangle a towing chain. I learned much elephant lore from a Burma teak planter, an elephant *wallah*. These observations became part of the day's "nourishment", a glimpse into a world both normal and harmonious.

It was in effect easier to find solace in the natural world than in human society. We never failed to crane our heads when the greater toucans flew above the canopy; if we couldn't see them, we heard the slow and powerful stroke of their wings. They were free, we thought.

Orchids and butterflies, exploding in evanescent bursts of colour, brought poignancy, even tenderness, into our lives. I once observed a butterfly in Tambaya, hovering above the bare foot of a corpse that had been laid out at the entrance of a hut. Its wings were shimmering with gold, yellow and Prussian blue. Exceptionally large, it was looking for a place to land on. It chose the corpse's big toe. The two polarities, the pale, inert flesh and the quivering insect, dissolved into one perception: in an instant as ephemeral as the flutter of gold on the butterfly's wings, I glimpsed the underlying unity of the world around me. Nothing was discrete from the whole, and simultaneously, I understood that I was seeing a reflection of my own mind.

Searching for quietude, I would walk off into the jungle, and sit in a small clearing. On rare occasions mind and body, kneaded by an involuntary ascetiscism, produced a tiny anthropocentric experience. The boundaries of self appeared to fuse with the non-self, and I entered into a brief and primal communion with my surroundings. In these moments of aloneness, I felt neither separateness, nor threat, nor hostility.

The captain had been right. When starved and worked to death in jungle camps, thoughts of home and freedom only served to widen the gap between the reality and the hope. Only the present counted, not the past nor the future. He had been right when he spoke of "nourishment", when at the end of the day it was still possible to say, "This I have seen, that I have heard."

Everything and every circumstance around us was utterly new and unexpected. We had been prepared for none of it. Not for our extraordinary habitat, the rain forest; not for our closeness to another people and its culture, the Japanese; and certainly not for the breakdown of our own group structure.

With its societal skin flayed, human nature became visible as never before. Greed, cowardice and vanity; perseverance, altruism and generosity, in brief the wide panoply of virtue and vice, were there to be observed in the open, without pretence, with no place to hide.

The captain, I found out later, died in Nikki. So, after all, if your luck had run out, neither "philosophy", nor help from your friends, nor even your own determination to keep on going were of much help. Your "number was up", as we used to say. Or *shikata ga nai*, to put it the Japanese way.

TWELVE

With the shrinking of the Japanese Empire, as one Pacific stronghold after another fell to the Americans, the attitude of the guards in Singapore changed. They now flaunted their ethnic origin. So far, our pretence was that we'd never heard of such a country as Korea.

"You know who I am," a guard would ask, offering a cigarette.

"You're Private Kanamoto."

"That's not my real name, you're aware of that? My real name is. . ." It was always Kim something. What they imagined had been kept secret from us for the last three years was at last revealed. And did we understand what it meant to be a Korean *heiho*, how much Koreans had suffered under the Nipponese yoke?

The preamble led to one of two possibilities: either it was taking out an insurance for the day when, after the Allied victory, accounts would be settled; or to request medical help, almost invariably M&B 693, the sulphonamide that would cure their venereal disease.

It was unfortunate that the guards knew we still had minute quantities of the medicine we had so carefully nurtured over the years. Even more worrisome was the source of their knowledge, most likely a medical orderly.

There was good reason for the guards to circumvent the I.J.A. medical services. Phase One of the V.D. cure was a sound thrashing. Phase Two consisted in the most painful treatment that Japanese research could devise, during which time the patient was assigned to disgusting fatigues. Simultaneously a notice appeared at the police station of the ward in Japan where the sufferer's family lived; it publicised that So-and-So, having contracted venereal disease while on active duty, had deprived His Majesty the Emperor of his services.

The only time we ever "sold" our sulphonamides was when we desperately needed something for the welfare of the camp. We used them for blackmail, but only with the Koreans. We hardly ever tried anything of that nature with the Japanese.

The Japanese themselves were getting edgy. Under the guise of discusssing their way of life and its contrast with ours, they might bring up the idiosyncrasy of linguistic expressions. *Mujoken kofuku*, unconditional surrender, they would say, was invented in Nippon-go strictly to apply to their enemies. Semantically, the proposition was irreversible, and there lay the proof that Japan would win the war. Some of my interlocutors, however, admitted that it might take a hundred years.

Given the intellectual apathy brought about by insufficient food (our rations were being cut down, and we were again desperately hungry), by boredom, and by a fearsome uncertainty as to how the end would come, there was little discussion of the Japanese enigma. For one thing, most of the prisoners found it convenient to give their captors a universal classification, most often that of 'subhuman fiends'. Yet I'm certain that each one of us had at least one exception which he called his "pet Nip". Every prisoner had, at some time, met a Japanese who'd been kind to him, and with whom he'd established friendly relations. These relations, it's hardly worth pointing out, were almost invariably based on the basic appetites common to all humanity.

The enigma, for me, was a culture that subsumed irreconcilable opposites. How was it possible to explain the Japanese sense of beauty inhabiting the same emotional pool as sadism, fanaticism and sentimentality? This sense of beauty, marked by the restraint and refinement of half-tones, wasn't often displayed: but then there may not have been much opportunity for its manifestation among the men of a railway building battalion locked in the jungle with their slaves. So when I came across it, the effect was all the more memorable. However infrequent among the Japanese, it was totally absent, or at least utterly invisible, on our side.

It was in the calmer atmosphere of Tambaya that I became conscious of that national characteristic. The branch with its perfect placement on the wall had left its mark. I tried to imagine the scene in a British, French or German barrack-room. No doubt the two men in question would have been accused of being "horrible queers", and told to take down that useless piece of wood which harboured bugs of all kinds.

We laughed at the Japanese comfort packages they received from home. We compared the paucity as well as the poverty of their contents with those of our own Red Cross packages (which, with one exception, never reached us – they were simply intercepted on arrival). Of these humble objects, a candle, a headband and *momme*, sweet soyabean paste, I remember how carefully and beautifully they were wrapped in coloured crêpe paper, housed in little wooden boxes or hidden in layers of patterned cotton,

Using split bamboo and oiled paper, the guards made storm-lanterns for their candles. The officer, the platoon's best educated man, traced with his brush a bold ideogram on one of the lantern's four faces.

I noticed the refinement. I was astonished, even moved. But it was only after my release that I became fully aware of the enigma. The pressures of life in the camps inhibited abstract thinking. Attention was directed to survival.

(1979)

I had brought two books on this journey. One I had recently found in Tokyo on my way to Bangkok. Entitled, *The Japanese*, and written by Professor Robert S. Ozaki, it purported to be 'a cultural portrait'. The other, which because of its bulk I had left on the raft, was Fosco Maraini's *Meeting with Japan*.

Maraini was interned by the Japanese after the Italian armistice of 1943, and he too asked how was it possible for a nation of poets and artists to produce in the members of its armed forces such callousness and cruelty.

For him, the root of the problem was the army's underlying obsession with the ancient ideal of the samurai. "You were born a samurai; you could not become one. A samurai's education was hard. He had to learn not to betray the slightest emotion, whether of joy, of fear; and learning the necessary degree of control took years. His word – *bushi-no ichi gon*, 'the single word of the warrior' – was sacred, and lying or deception (*ni-gon*) meant death."

The samurai was long gone, a warrior about whom Maraini also says that "there was only one thing which [he] must not understand, and that was the use of money. The sign of a really good education was inability to recognise the various coins in current circulation. A samurai would often work in his fields with the peasants, but he was rigorously forbidden to take part in trade." The armed forces of modern Japan were made up of the farmers, factory workers, clerks, and functionaries that form the backbone of any industrial society. The samurai code was as removed from the stuff of their daily lives as the rules of jousting are to a football team. Yet, as soon as they were given their uniform, they discovered that the ethos of their existence had brutally changed; they were obliged to subsume their private and diverse views of the world and of their own life. Without transition, and without prior training, they were forced to transform themselves into an archaic creature motivated by "courage [and] valour combined with serenity and composure".

To mark the change clearly, the ceremony of induction into the armed forces signified that the recruit had effectively donated his life to the service of the Emperor. When and how and where his life would be taken away from him was an academic matter.

We had seen on the march up how far Japanese troops would push themselves, the extent of their endurance and their capacity for suffering. And in Thanbyuzayat, the cruelty of their training. All along, we had witnessed (and experienced) the face slappings which were passed on, in a descending scale, from one rank to another.

Maraini's argument is that because man's nature is to avoid suffering, and when it is inflicted, to reject it in a classic transference, the unbearable stress and pain caused by the samurai transformation were passed on to those who could not hit back.

If this is the explanation for the mental instability of the Japanese forces, their gratuitous violence and their self-enforced masochism, it fails to account for another phenomenon: the uniform behaviour, for good or for bad, observable within a given *butai*, any integrated unit of the I.J.A. Putting aside the Koreans, who had to contend with their own problems, we have seen the Engineers being uniformly callous to their prisoners, while the combat troops of the two platoons that guarded us at Tambaya behaved in an exemplary fashion. It was bewildering to see how troops conformed to the image of their immediate superior, not so much out of discipline but because of what appeared to be a collective will to which they subordinated their individual passions.

In Professor Ozaki's book I found an idea that approached the problem from another direction.

His concern is to describe a state of being and the mainspring of action, rather than to account for a mechanistic process, in effect a chain of psychological causality. It is no explanation, of course, any more than Carl Jung's observation of Teutonic archetypes making their appearances in his patients' dreams is an explanation for the emergence of Nazism.

"What motivates the Japanese," writes Professor Ozaki, "is tension and not ideological fortitude. In the most fundamental sense, their philosophy is the belief in nonbelief." This is followed by the key for the understanding of the Engineers' attitude: "What matters is that you mobilize all your resources toward action, giving little attention to the critical reasons for and consequences of your action."

In their furious zeal, the two Railway Building Battalions fused into one collective being bent on one task. Like the samurai's cry from the pit of the stomach as he brings his sword down, the terrible shout, "Speedo!", created the tension. As for the irrational destruction of the Engineers' own manpower, prisoners and native levies, Ozaki's argument fits perfectly.

Before meeting the Japanese, we had thought of them in stereotypes which, in spite of their grotesque contents, we never questioned. In the course of three-and-a-half years, not only were these sterotypes destroyed, but we had observed that our captors' attitudes, even their innate nature, were extraordinarily varied.

This made it impossible, or at least very difficult, to try and draw a profile of the "leading race" *(shido minzoku)*, as they sometimes referred to themselves. Any theory or any attempt to discern a pattern based on personal experience could instantly be countered by an equally potent argument, also derived from personal contact. The same difficulty, it would appear, has faced the many writers, anthropologists, social scientists, historians or

170

long-time residents in the country, who have addressed themselves to the Japanese "problem."

If, back in Singapore, those of us who had been with F Force never asked aloud "Why am I still alive?", there were many questions about the Japanese that we tossed to each other like a ball. But we never found a convincing answer.

We couldn't, for instance, reconcile the Japanese soldier's valour, his endurance of pain, his capacity for self-sacrifice and his courage, with his lamentable attitude to sickness. An attack of malaria released moans, complaints and a stream of self-pity. He was trained to receive man-inflicted wounds with equanimity, and to face death calmly. But the decay of the body was unacceptable.

The fear of contagion among our guards was pathological. It was the mixture of awe and repulsion they had for human remains that made it possible to hide with a measure of safety the notes I wrote in 1943. I placed them in a hollow bamboo half-filled with ashes, and, had I ever been challenged, I would have said that they were my best friend's ashes.

When in 1944 a trainload of Japanese troops, sick and wounded, stopped at Konkuita, on their way back from the Burma front, they were kept shut up for hours without food or water. The prisoners, moved by pity, requested permission to help them. It was the prisoners who brought them food and water, even parting with some of their tobacco. Their own people refused to have anything to do with them, perhaps because they belonged to another *butai*, another unit, for the cohesion and the strength of a Japanese military unit were based on a rejection of all other units.

But then what happened to that cohesion when, in Nikki, a Japanese who contracted cholera was abandoned by his comrades? He was removed to the prisoners' cholera hut, and prisoners nursed him.

What are we to make of the kind interpreter-captain who was the first to commit suicide when he heard the Imperial Rescript and the defeat of his country?

And of the abject Toyama whose reaction, although he was a Korean *gunsoku*, was also typical of the Engineers? Cyril Wild, the senior interpreter, once asked him: "What have these prisoners done that they should be beaten?"

"They are prisoners. That's enough," answered Toyama.

"Amongst us, we consider it cowardly to hit a man who cannot hit back."

Toyama shouted, "Are you calling me a coward?"

"We know nothing about you," said Wild. "We have never seen you. But today you are acting like a coward."

White with rage, Toyama said: "How can I get them to do what I want if I don't beat them?"

And what of the cadet who invited Hutch and myself to his tea-party, and never mentioned the "close shave" of the day?

Lastly: how can we account for Banno's tears when Harris told him we had trusted the I.J.A.'s promises, and so many of us were now dead?

THIRTEEN

In July 1945 I was still in Kranji. Every fit man who could be spared from hospital duties was roped in by the Japanese to build earthworks in preparation for the expected invasion of Singapore by the British.

A Korean guard came to visit me with dramatic news. His brother, who worked in the offices of the Malay P.O.W. Administration, had seen orders for the massacre of all prisoners on Singapore Island. On the morning of August 15, trucks were to come and take us to the beaches where we would be machine-gunned. Wherever there were P.O.W.s, he added, specific instructions had been laid down to eliminate them in the event of enemy action. The I.J.A. couldn't spare troops for guarding prisoners, nor did they want to be threatened in their rear.

At the Kranji hospital we had to decide whether we would stick by the sick, fight it out with staves and knives, and all be killed; or whether we should opt for a *sauve-qui-peut*, and hope a few would get away. We chose the latter.

On the evening of August 6, I was sitting in my hut, depressed and apprehensive about the future. The camp commandant, a regular army sergeant, was unstable, and often, I believed, uncomfortably close to *musekinin*. I could now see signs of hysteria, and there was little doubt that he'd been informed of the morning program for the 15th.

A friend who was in charge of the underground radio came to see me.

"Listen," he said, sensing my mood, "I'm ready to have a bet with you: tonight, we'll hear fantastic news. I feel it."

I replied that even the invasion of the main islands of Japan was no solution to the problem facing us in a week's time.

But I accepted his bet. I proposed the best dinner we could get in London.

At two a.m., he entered my hut again, and slipped his head under the mosquito netting.

"You owe me a fantastic dinner," he whispered. He tried to describe a device called an atom bomb that had devastated Hiroshima. We made wild calculations: how many bombs were needed to destroy half the Japanese population. It could be done with a score or two. We never gave a thought to the destruction of millions of civilians. All that mattered was that we were saved, for it was unthinkable that the military in Singapore would go ahead with the planned massacre.

The second bomb was dropped on Nagasaki. The guards were aware that something was happening. They didn't know what, and they were not allowed into town. Our sergeant was swinging between hysteria and numb silence.

Japan surrendered on the U.S.S. *Missouri* in Tokyo Bay. We were still prisoners. Night and day we were still building fortifications.

On August 22 a guard came to tell me that Hutch and I were to report immediately to the camp office, where Colonel Banno had arrived. Banno stood up when we entered, saluted and told us to be seated.

"I have grave news for you," he said. "Japan and the Allies have signed an armistice. That doesn't mean that the war is over: it could start again. But for the time being, you are allowed certain privileges. Tell me what you need."

Hutch had understood pretty well, but this wasn't the moment to change three years of routine. I translated, making tremendous efforts not to break out into an uncontrollable giggle.

Hutch said he wanted a moment's reflection. The two of us sat in a corner to decide on a priority of requests. I said that we must have the sergeant removed immediately. I feared an irrational act. We then asked for drugs, food and clothing. That very afternoon, trucks started rolling in and the sergeant left the camp.

The Japanese garrison soon found out that the 'armistice' had been transformed into *mujoken kofuku*, unconditional surrender. They didn't commit mass suicide, and they didn't even seem terribly concerned, except for their Occupation Dollars; they swarmed into Singapore Town and they bought everything that the Chinese would sell them in exchange for their paper money.

Mountbatten had given orders that the Japanese garrison on the island was to move to Johore, on the mainland, in order to minimise the risk of an armed clash when the British forces landed.

For two days, from our camp in Kranji, we saw them trudging along the road leading to the Causeway and Johore – 125,000 Japanese troops laden down under the weight of their gear, defeated without firing a shot by order of their Emperor, and on their way to becoming prisoners-of-war.

From behind the barbed-wire, the survivors of three and a half years watched them go by.

No one jeered, no one whistled, no one gloated. But I heard a man say, "Poor bastards. Now it's their turn to be caught in the big fuckin' machine."

Toyama, the Korean *heiho*, was hanged in Changi in 1947. So was Lieutenant Abe, the head of the Engineers at Sonkurai.

Colonel Banno was sentenced to three years' imprisonment.

In 1981, the barrage that was under construction at Tha-Kahanun was completed. Now the waters of the Mae Nam Kwae Noi have spread over the river basin all the way to Sangkla Buri obliterating much of the country described in this memoir.